# English for
## Oil & Gas

**Vocational English**
**Course Book**

Evan Frendo with David Bonamy

Series editor David Bonamy

# Contents

Contents

# 1 People and jobs

- talk about roles and responsibilities
- explain an oil rig's organisation
- describe work routines
- discuss transportation

## Roles and responsibilities

**Reading**  **1**  Read the information and match words 1–4 to photos A–D.

1 geophysicist  2 lab technician  3 production engineer  4 roughneck

**A** I work in the downstream sector of the industry, in a refinery. We manufacture a wide range of products for domestic and industrial uses, such as lubricants, bitumen, liquefied petroleum gas (LPG) and petrochemicals. ☐

**B** I work on an offshore oil rig. I spend a lot of my time tripping drill pipe in and out of the hole, and operating the tongs to make or break connections. I also do other jobs around the rig, such as looking after equipment. ☐

**C** I look at seismic data and help the company make decisions about where to drill. At the moment we are looking at a shale gas reservoir in the USA. Shale gas is natural gas found in shale formations. ☐

**D** I work for an E&P independent. I'm part of the team of people responsible for the operation, production and maintenance of different facilities in this area. My main job is to find the best way to bring the oil to the surface. ☐

**Vocabulary**  **2**  Match words 1–6 to definitions a–f.

| | |
|---|---|
| 1 downstream sector | a) put a pipe in/pull a pipe out of a drill hole |
| 2 LPG | b) activities to do with refining, transportation, sales and marketing |
| 3 trip in/out | c) connected with earth vibration |
| 4 E&P independent | d) independent exploration and production company |
| 5 seismic | e) liquefied petroleum gas |
| 6 shale gas | f) natural gas found in a type of sedimentary rock |

lube oil =
lubricating oil

**3** 🔘 **02** Listen to four conversations. Are these statements *true* (T) or *false* (F)?

**Conversation 1**
1 Lab technicians mix oils and additives. (T / F)
2 Customers come to the refinery and pump oil from the storage tanks. (T / F)

**Conversation 2**
3 Roustabouts don't work in the rain. (T / F)
4 Roustabouts work alone. (T / F)

**Conversation 3**
5 Production engineers work in offices all day. (T / F)
6 Production engineers have to follow health and safety procedures. (T / F)

**Conversation 4**
7 The layers of rock reflect shock waves. (T / F)
8 Geophysicists analyse seismic data. (T / F)

**4** Answer these questions. Then listen again and check your answers.
1 What does the lab technician optimise?
2 Does a roustabout clean and paint?
3 Is production engineering a technical job?
4 What do vibrator trucks do?

**Language**

| Present simple | |
|---|---|
| We use the **present simple** to talk about facts, repeated actions and habits. | *Geophysicists **analyse** seismic data.*<br>*We **manufacture** a wide range of products.*<br>*Roustabouts **don't work** alone.* |
| *Yes/No questions* | ***Do** you **work** in a crew?*<br>***Is** it an easy job?* |
| *Wh- questions* | *What **do** you **do**?*<br>*Where **do** you **work**?*<br>*Who **does** she **work** for?* |

**5** Put this conversation in the correct order.

☐ B: Yes, I do. I stand on the monkey board at the top of the derrick. I guide the drill pipe when we trip out or in. I'm also responsible for the fluid pumps and the circulation system.

☐ B: Yes, it is. But I know what I'm doing and I'm careful.

☐ A: A derrickhand? So do you work high up?

1 A: What do you do, Adel?

☐ B: I'm a derrickhand on an oil rig.

☐ A: Isn't that dangerous?

**6** Read the conversation in 5 again. Write a paragraph about Adel.

*Adel is a derrickhand on an oil rig. He … .*

**Speaking** **7** Work in pairs. Choose an oil industry job you are familiar with. Explain the job to your partner.

*Roustabouts work on oil rigs. They do jobs like cleaning … .*

# The organisation

Read the text and complete this organisation chart with the job titles in the box.

hand = a crew
member who does
physical work

derrickhand    driller    drilling engineer    motorhand
mud engineer    roughnecks    roustabouts    toolpusher

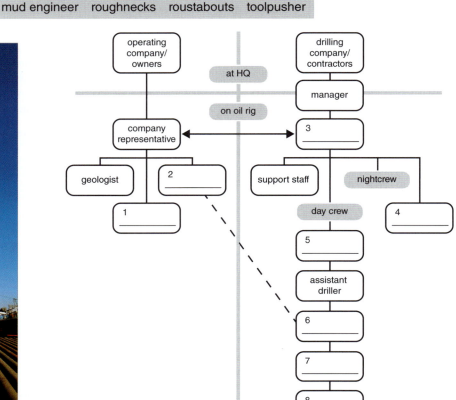

# A guide to jobs on an oil rig

## Employees of the exploration or operating company

- **Company representative:** Works for the operating or exploration company. Can give instructions to the toolpusher but does not directly supervise the toolpusher or the drilling crews.

- **Drilling engineer:** Specialises in the technical aspects of drilling. Reports to the company representative.

- **Mud/Drilling fluids engineer:** Responsible for the drilling fluid. Reports to the company representative.

## Employees of the drilling company contractors

- **Toolpusher:** Manages the drilling crews on the rig and the support staff. Can receive instructions from the company representative but reports to the manager of the drilling contractor company.

- **Driller:** Supervises a drilling crew. Controls the rig's machinery during the drilling operation. Has an assistant driller.

- **Derrickhand:** Handles the top of the drill string when the crew are tripping it in or out of the well hole. Also responsible for the flow of drilling fluid into and out of the well hole. Reports to the assistant driller and works closely with the mud engineer.

- **Roughnecks:** Skilled workers on the floor of the rig. Operate the tongs to make up and break out drill strings. Also trip pipe in and out of the well hole. Report to the derrickhand.

- **Roustabouts:** Semi-skilled workers. Do most of the painting and cleaning jobs on the rig. Report to the roughnecks.

- **Motorhand:** Responsible for the maintenance and operation of drilling engines and motors. Acts as a mechanic and an electrician. Reports to the toolpusher.

**2** Look at the organisation chart and text in 1 again. Answer these questions.

1 Who is responsible for the drilling fluid?
2 Who looks after the engines?
3 Who represents the operating or exploration company?
4 Who does the painting and cleaning jobs?
5 Who reports to the manager of the drilling contractor company?
6 Who supervises the drilling crew?
7 Who operates the tongs?

**Vocabulary 3** Complete this table with words from the text in 1. Which nouns refer to people?

| Noun | Verb |
|---|---|
| 1 _____ | maintain |
| supervisor | 2 _____ |
| 3 _____ | instruct |
| operation | 4 _____ |
| 5 _____ | drill |
| 6 _____ | assist |
| manager | 7 _____ |
| 8 _____ | represent |
| 9 _____ | explore |

**4** Complete these sentences with the correct form of words from 3.

1 The company _____ works for the _____ company.
2 As a motorhand, I'm responsible for the _____ and _____ of all the engines.
3 My job is to support the driller. I'm his _____ .
4 Each driller _____ one of the crews.
5 In some places the toolpusher is called the rig _____ .

**Listening 5** 🔊 03 Listen to Abdul as he introduces Harish to the rig crew. What is Harish's job and where will he work?

**6** Listen again. Match the names to the job titles.

1 Mr J        a) motorhand
2 John        b) driller
3 Mohammed    c) toolpusher
4 Ali         d) drilling engineer
5 Samir       e) company representative
6 Abdul       f) mud/drilling fluids engineer

**Speaking 7** Work in pairs. Choose and complete one of the following tasks.

1 Draw an organisation chart for your own school or organisation. Explain it to your partner.
2 Make a list of different job titles in your school or organisation. Explain the jobs to your partner.

# Work routines

**1** Work in pairs. What is the app in photo A for? What about the software in photo B? Discuss with a partner.

A

B Schedule View

| File | Edit | View | Help |

| New Schedule | Delete Schedule | Print Schedule |

| Name | Thu 14/6 | Fr 15/6 | Sa 16/6 | Su 17/6 | Mo 18/6 |
|---|---|---|---|---|---|
| S Bowler | | | | | |
| E Hill | | | | | |
| H Schwarz | | | | | |
| D LeBlanc | | | | | |
| A Fox | | | | | |

**Listening** **2** 🔘 04 Listen to three conversations and answer these questions.

1 Where do the speakers in conversation 1 work?
2 Where does the woman in conversation 2 work?
3 Where does the man in conversation 3 work?

**3** Complete these sentences with the words in the box. Then listen again and check your answers.

> call clock downtime reschedule routine set shifts straight

1 On this rig, workers are on the job for 12 hours a day for seven _____ days.
2 The night _____ were the worst.
3 For _____ tests, we take samples at specific times from specific locations, according to a _____ schedule.
4 Last week we had a problem with some of the crude inflow, so we had to _____ all our tests.
5 I'm on _____ 24 hours a day.
6 Everything had to be planned properly to minimise _____ .
7 We had to work around the _____ to complete the job.

**Vocabulary** **4** Match phrases 1–7 to definitions a–g.

1 out of the ordinary
2 week-long break
3 around the clock
4 reschedule
5 on call
6 seven days on
7 the night shift

a) available for work
b) unexpected or non-routine
c) seven days off work
d) day and night without stopping
e) make a new timetable/schedule
f) working from sunset to sunrise
g) working for a week

**Language**

**Past simple**

|  | Regular verbs | Irregular verbs |
|---|---|---|
| We use the **past simple** to talk about a completed action in the past. | He **called** me an hour ago.<br>He **didn't call** me.<br>**Did** he **call** you?<br>When **did** he **call** you? | They **had** a problem yesterday.<br>They **didn't have** a problem yesterday.<br>**Did** they **have** a problem yesterday?<br>What kind of problem **did** they **have** yesterday? |

**5** Complete this conversation with the past simple form of the verbs in the box.

> finish   use   want   you/have   you/see

Ahmed:  Ahmed Bin Mohammed.
Kevin:   Hi, Ahmed. It's Kevin.
Ahmed:  Hi, Kevin. What's up?
Kevin:   I just wanted to say that we (1) _____ the repairs an hour ago.
Ahmed:  That's excellent news. (2) _____ any problems?
Kevin:   No, not really. We (3) _____ some of the off-shift crew for a couple of hours.
Ahmed:  OK. (4) _____ Joe yesterday? He (5) _____ to give you some documents.
Kevin:   No, I didn't. I'll catch him tomorrow in the office.
Ahmed:  Sounds good. OK. Thanks for calling.
Kevin:   You're welcome. Bye, Ahmed.
Ahmed:  Bye.

**Reading**  **6** Read this text about a refinery shutdown and answer the questions.

Normally, the refinery runs 24 hours a day, seven days a week but last week was different. The refinery was on a scheduled shutdown in order to inspect, upgrade and clean our equipment. We also replaced one of the coke coolers. Over a thousand extra contractors came in to do this maintenance work, so we had a lot of extra traffic, especially during shift changes. This sort of turnaround maintenance takes place every four to five years.

1  Why was the refinery shut down last week?
2  Was the shutdown planned?
3  What type of equipment was changed?
4  Why was there extra traffic?
5  How often does the refinery shut down for turnaround maintenance?

**Speaking**  **7** Work in pairs. Explain what you typically do each week over a period of one month.

*A couple of weeks ago was very typical. I was on night shift the whole week, so I started work at … .*

# Transport to site

**Vocabulary** **1** Label these photos with the words in the box.

> helicopter   low loader   tracked vehicle   transfer basket

**Reading** **2** Read these comments by oil workers and underline the words for forms of transport. Which comments refer to the types of transport in 1?

1   'The rig camp is in the middle of the Omani desert. It takes several hours to get to the location. First, a taxi to the airport. Then, an early flight to the oil industry base at Fahud, normally in a propeller aircraft. And then two hours by crew bus.'

2   'I'm a driller on an exploration platform in the Campos basin, which is a large oil field off Rio de Janeiro. Every day approximately 2,000 workers fly by helicopter from the mainland to the platforms in the area, so it's very busy. Sometimes there are delays due to bad weather but normally the total travel time from hotel to rig is about four hours.'

3   'I'm a roustabout on a production rig which is quite close to the shore, so we travel by crew boat. The total distance is only about 600 m. When we get to the rig, the operator lowers the transfer basket and hoists us up.'

4   'I work on pipeline repairs. We use different vehicles to get to the work site, depending on the type of ground we have to cover. Our fleet has both wheeled and tracked vehicles, with payload capacities up to 40 tons. For long distances we use low loaders to transport the vehicles.'

5   'I'm a chemist in a refinery just outside the town where I live. It takes me 20 minutes by bicycle to get from my home to my office. On rainy days I take my car. The refinery is at the mouth of the river, on the south bank. You often see oil tankers there.'

**Vocabulary** **3** Match 1–5 to a–e to make forms of transport.

1   low
2   crew
3   tracked
4   propeller
5   oil

a) vehicle
b) loader
c) tanker
d) bus
e) aircraft

## Language

| Describing location | |
|---|---|
| We use a number of different phrases to describe short distances. The meaning is similar. | *The refinery is **just outside/quite close to** the town.* *My office is **quite close to** Main Street.* *The oil field is **just off** the coast.* |
| We can use different phrases to say where things are. | *The airport is **in the middle of** the desert.* *The jetty is **on the south bank of** the river.* *The rig is **at the mouth of** the river.* |

**4** Read the sentences in the Language box and write the names of the places for A–F on this map.

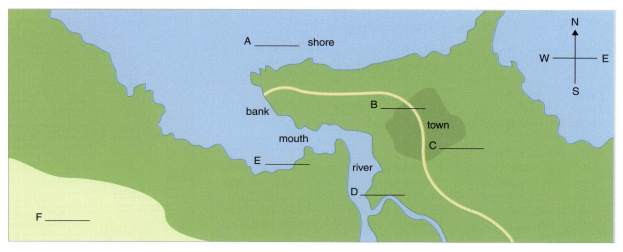

**5** Match 1–7 to a–g to make sentences.

| | | | |
|---|---|---|---|
| 1 | The oil field is in the middle | a) | the mouth of the river. |
| 2 | The oil field is | b) | to the shore. |
| 3 | The distance is | c) | of the desert. |
| 4 | The rig is close | d) | off Rio de Janeiro. |
| 5 | The refinery is just outside | e) | the town. |
| 6 | The refinery is at | f) | south bank of the river. |
| 7 | The refinery is on the | g) | about 600 m. |

**Listening 6** ▶ **05** Look at this map. Then listen to a conversation and label the rigs, the harbour and the refinery.

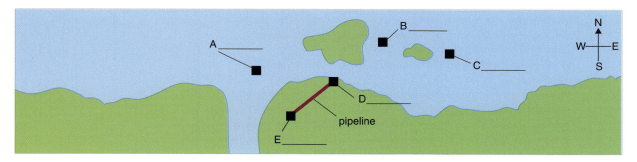

**Speaking 7** Work in pairs. Discuss the different types of transport you use to get to your place of work/study.

# Procedures

- read and understand safety rules and regulations
- explain decontamination procedures
- follow load handling instructions
- describe hazards at the place of work

## Rules and regulations

**Reading**  **1** Read this accident report. Then read the safety poster and tick ✓ the safety rules which were broken.

---

### Accident report

**Date:**       13 October
**Time:**      1742Z
**Location:**  drilling rig Alpha 341

<u>Description of incident</u>

John Brown (motorhand) was injured when his fall protection lanyard was caught and wrapped around a rotating kelly bar. According to Brown, this is what happened: he completed some work in the derrick using a full body harness. His lanyard was attached to the D-ring on the back of the harness. He climbed down and detached the lanyard from the lifeline but did not remove the harness or the lanyard from his body. Then he walked across the rig floor, near to the rotating kelly. The lanyard was caught by the kelly and Brown was pulled towards the moving parts. Fortunately, another man (Kevin Watts) quickly pressed the emergency stop button.

<u>Description of injuries</u>

---

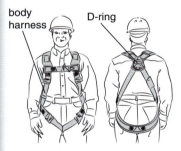

body harness / D-ring

## Safety rules on an offshore rig

1. ☐ The rig must have a temporary safe refuge (TSR), or safe room, a safe escape route to the sea and a safe route to the lifeboats.
2. ☐ A safety boat must always be on standby near the platform, to rescue people who fall into the sea.
3. ☐ Workers must not enter the danger zone when the rotary table is in motion.
4. ☐ Workers must remove fall protection equipment, such as lanyards, immediately when it is not needed.
5. ☐ Workers must remove or confine loose clothing, long hair, jewellery, watches, etc.
6. ☐ Workers must not bring dangerous items, such as matches, lighters or other flammable items aboard offshore oil rigs.
7. ☐ Before coming aboard an offshore oil rig, all luggage must be checked.
8. ☐ Every piece of equipment on the offshore oil rig must be tested regularly.
9. ☐ When equipment is tested, it must be identified with a colour code.
10. ☐ Workers must not use equipment with an out-of-date colour code.

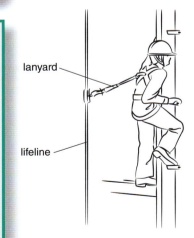

lanyard

lifeline

**2** Match 1–7 to a–g to make collocations.

| | | | |
|---|---|---|---|
| 1 | loose | a) | route |
| 2 | fall | b) | protection |
| 3 | safety | c) | zone |
| 4 | escape | d) | clothing |
| 5 | danger | e) | code |
| 6 | rotary | f) | boat |
| 7 | colour | g) | table |

**3** Complete these sentences with the collocations in 2.

1 The visitor's _____ was caught in the _____ .
2 The _____ was waiting near the platform.
3 The new roustabout forgot his _____ equipment.
4 Do not use equipment with an out-of-date _____ .
5 The _____ went from the _____ to the sea.

**4** ▶ 🔊 06 Listen, write the words you hear and underline the word stress. Then find the words in the safety poster in 1.

1 *jewellery*
2 _____
3 _____
4 _____
5 _____

**Language**

## The passive

| We often use **the passive** in written English. To transform an active sentence into a passive sentence, we use this pattern:<br>subject of the passive sentence (object of the active sentence) + *to be* + past participle + *by* + agent (the doer of the action, the subject of the active sentence). | Active:<br>*The rotating kelly **injured** the motorhand.*<br>Passive:<br>*The motorhand **was injured by** the rotating kelly.* |
|---|---|
| It is not always necessary to include *by* + agent. | *The motorhand **was injured**.* |
| We use the passive: | |
| • to focus on what happened, not on who or what performed an action. | *The equipment **is tested** regularly.*<br>*The lanyard **was caught**.* |
| • when the doer of the action is self-evident or not important. | *This equipment **is made** in Germany.*<br>*The well **was drilled** last week.* |
| • to talk about processes. | *The kelly **is fixed** to the drill pipe. Then the drill string **is tripped** into the well hole.* |

**5** Rewrite these sentences in the passive.

1 The rotary table caught the derrickhand's lanyard.
2 The visitor wore loose clothing.
3 The toolpusher reported the accident.
4 The engineer pressed the emergency stop button.
5 The driller supervised the workers.
6 A company in Germany makes these tools.
7 The security guard checks the luggage.

**6** Work in pairs. Discuss accidents you have seen or heard about. Was anyone injured? Were any safety rules broken?

# Decontamination procedures

**Vocabulary**   **1**   Label photos A–E with the words in the box.

> cloth hose   contaminated water   porous material
> soiled gloves   steam cleaning

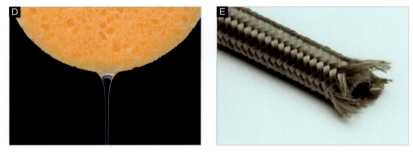

**2**   Complete this extract from a company's standard operating procedures (SOPs) with the words in the box.

> bits   cleaned   minimise   porous   soiled   water

## PROCEDURES

### Drilling equipment cleaning and decontamination

**1** Prior to departure, the drill rig and all drilling equipment should be thoroughly _____ to remove all oil, grease, mud, etc.

**2** Before each drilling operation, all downhole drill equipment, the rig and other equipment should be steam cleaned or cleaned using high pressure hot _____ and rinsed with pressurised potable water to _____ cross-contamination.

**3** Equipment with _____ surfaces, such as rope, cloth hoses and wooden blocks or tool handles, cannot be thoroughly decontaminated. These should be disposed of properly.

**4** Cleaned equipment should not be handled with _____ gloves. Surgical gloves, new clean cotton work gloves or other appropriate gloves should be used and disposed of, even when only slightly soiled.

**5** The use of newly painted drill _____ and tools should be avoided, since paint chips will likely be introduced into the monitoring system.

**Listening**

**3** ▶ 🔊 07 Listen to a supervisor explaining decontamination procedures to a new employee. Match these procedures (a–e) to the supervisor's instructions.

a) Clean the drill rig and all drilling equipment prior to departure. __
b) Steam clean the equipment, then rinse with potable water. __
c) Dispose of equipment with porous surfaces. __
d) Dispose of soiled gloves. __
e) Do not use newly painted tools or equipment. __

**4** Listen to conversations 1–3 again. Write words that match these definitions.

1  prior to      _____
2  rinse         _____
3  potable       _____
4  dispose of    _____
5  soiled        _____

**Vocabulary**

**5** Complete these sentences with the words in the box. There is one extra word.

> away   cleaned   cleaner   cleaning   mud   water

1  This equipment should be thoroughly _____ .
2  First, use the steam _____ .
3  Remove all the grease and _____ .
4  Then wash the equipment with potable _____ .
5  Don't forget to throw the old ropes _____ .

**Language**

| **Should and must** | |
|---|---|
| We use **should** to make recommendations or suggestions. | You **should clean** the drill bits first. <br> You **shouldn't wear** jewellery. |
| We use **must** for rules. *Must* is stronger than *should*. | You **must use** the steam cleaner. <br> You **mustn't wear** soiled gloves. |
| *Should* and *must* can also be used in the passive (*must/should + be + past participle*). | Active: You **should/must clean** the drill bits. <br> Passive: The drill bits **should/must be cleaned**. |

**6** Complete these sentences with the correct active or passive form of *should* .

1  You _____ (remove) the contamination.
2  _____ (we/steam clean) the drill pipes next?
3  Contaminated cloth hoses _____ (dispose) of.
4  You _____ (avoid) newly painted drill bits.
5  All this equipment _____ (clean) using high pressure hot water.

**Speaking**

**7** Work in pairs. Discuss procedures for cleaning equipment you are familiar with.

A: *I use a steam cleaner quite often.*
B: *Really? What do you use it for?*
A: *To clean the workshop floor.*
B: *What's the procedure?*
A: *Well, first we normally sweep the floor. And we put any tools away.*
B: *OK.*
A: *Then we … .*

# Load handling instructions

**1** Label illustrations A and B with the words in the box.

> block   container   hook   load   wire rope

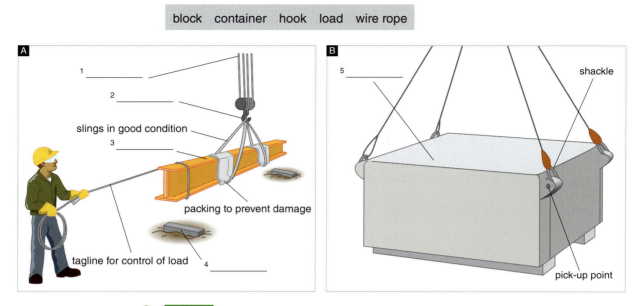

A
1 _____
2 _____
slings in good condition
3 _____
packing to prevent damage
tagline for control of load
4 _____

B
5 _____
shackle
pick-up point

**Listening** **2** 🔊 08 Listen to a supervisor (S) giving instructions to a roustabout (R) and complete their conversation.

S: Right, now let me give you some general rules about working with (1) _____ . Listen carefully. First of all, make sure the work area is clear. If there's an obstruction, (2) _____ it. And by obstruction I mean anything which shouldn't be there: tools, equipment, boxes – you name it. OK?

R: OK.

S: Good. Next, always (3) _____ the condition of the equipment. If you see any damage, just (4) _____ me. For example, corroded or broken (5) _____ ropes or worn slings. That kind of thing is very dangerous. Understand?

R: Yes, OK.

S: Always use taglines to control a load. If a load swings to the left or right, you just (6) _____ it back. And another thing: attach (7) _____ or shackles to pick-up points. If there are no pick-up points, use slings and packing to prevent damage.

R: Got it.

S: Now, do you know the emergency stop signal?

R: Yes. Like this?

S: Yes, exactly. Well, if you see a problem, (8) _____ the signal.

R: OK.

S: Oh, yeah. If you aren't a qualified rigger, you mustn't rig loads.

R: Aha, OK.

S: And finally, if you don't understand your task, (9) _____ the person in charge.

**3** Listen again and tick ✓ the topics that are mentioned.

1 ☐ transport       4 ☐ equipment       6 ☐ stop signals
2 ☐ taglines        5 ☐ clothing         7 ☐ cleanliness
3 ☐ obstructions

**Vocabulary**  **4**  Label photos A–E with words and phrases from the conversation in 2.

_____   _____   _____

_____   _____

**Language**

**If + present simple + imperative**

We can use the conditional structure **if + present simple + imperative** to give instructions. When the sentence starts with *if*, we put a comma after the *if* clause.

**If** you **see** some damage, **tell** your supervisor./**Tell** your supervisor **if** you **see** some damage.
**If** you **don't understand** your task, **ask** the person in charge./**Ask** the person in charge **if** you **don't understand** your task.

**5**  Match 1–5 to a–e to make sentences.

1  If you don't know,
2  If the load swings to the left,
3  If there is a problem,
4  If your gloves are soiled,
5  If the equipment is dirty,

a)  pull it to the right.
b)  throw them away.
c)  ask.
d)  clean it.
e)  give the emergency stop signal.

**6**  Complete these sentences.

1  If you see a fire, _____ .
2  If you are hungry or thirsty, _____ .
3  If you want to speak better English, _____ .

**Speaking**  **7**  Work in pairs. Student A, look at the information on this page. Student B, look at the information on page 76. Follow the instructions.

**Student A**
You are a supervisor. Practise the conversation in 2 with Student B. Then swap roles and repeat the activity. Remember to discuss the following:
• obstructions   • stop signals   • taglines   • condition of equipment

# Hazards

**1** Match words 1–10 to illustrations A–J.

1 falling hammer
2 mouse hole
3 obstructions
4 short monkeyboard
5 swinging kelly

6 missing guard rail
7 moving pipes
8 rotating kelly
9 steps and rungs
10 tong handle

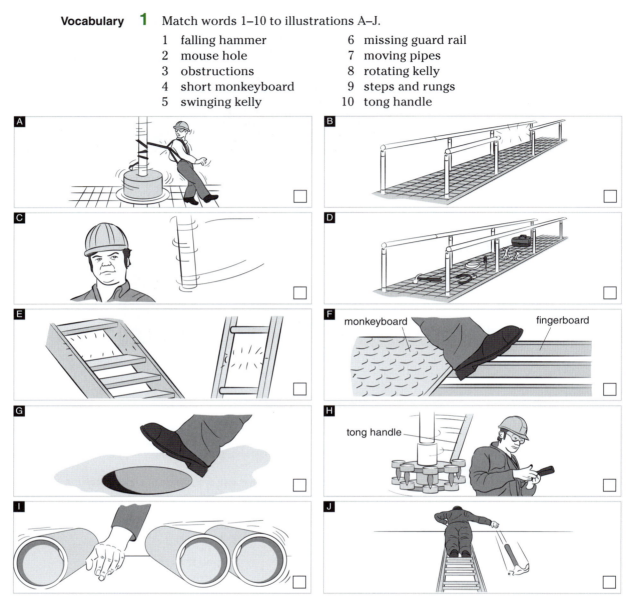

**Reading** **2** Match hazards 1–10 to illustrations A–J in 1.

## Safety hazards on an oil rig

**1** If there are obstructions in the walkway, you might trip or fall over them. ___

**2** If you carry tools when you are climbing, you might drop them on someone. ___

**3** If rungs are missing from a stairway or ladder, you could fall from a height. ___

**4** The rotating kelly might catch your loose clothing. ___

**5** A kelly or pipe could swing and strike your head. ___

**6** If a guard rail is missing from a walkway, you could fall off. ___

**7** If you step off a monkeyboard onto a fingerboard, you might fall off. ___

**8** Moving pipes could trap your hand and crush it. ___

**9** When the handle of the tong swings, it might strike you. ___

**10** You could fall into an uncovered mouse hole. ___

**3**   🔊 **09**   Listen to three conversations. Choose the hazard you hear.

1   a) wet rung          b) broken rung          c) missing rung
2   a) missing           b) broken               c) twisted
       monkeyboard            monkeyboard             monkeyboard
3   a) loose clothing    b) helicopter landing pad   c) helicopter rotor

**4**   Listen again. What exactly happened in each situation?

**Language**

| *Might* **and** *could* | |
|---|---|
| We use **_might_** and **_could_** to say there is a possibility of something happening. | You **_might_** fall over an obstruction.<br>The pipes **_could_** trap your hand. |
| We can also use **_might_** and **_could_** in conditional sentences. We use *if* + present simple + *might/could* + infinitive. | **_If_** we **_get_** bad weather, we **_might stop_** work. |

**5**   Match 1–5 to a–e to make short exchanges.

1   If it rains, you might get wet.
2   If the pipes arrive late, we might have to delay the drilling.
3   If the weather gets worse, we could be in for a rough night.
4   Could you make the tea?
5   Do you know where the incident file is?

a) No, sorry. But John might know.
b) Yes, the sea is quite high already.
c) The company rep won't like that.
d) Yes, but only if I forget my raincoat.
e) No, sorry. I made it yesterday. Your turn today.

**Writing**   **6**   Use these notes to write a report.

*guard rail on stairway missing – no guards on winch – 3 drillers with no hard hats – nuts and bolts missing from swivel – no cables for tools – walkway blocked with hoses*

## Safety report

I inspected the oil rig on 24 August and I observed these safety hazards:

**1** A guard rail on a stairway was missing.

**2** There were no _____ .

**3** Three drillers did not _____ .

**4** _____ .

**5** _____ .

**6** _____ .

**Speaking**   **7**   Work in pairs. Make a list of hazards in your place of work/study. Discuss what could happen.

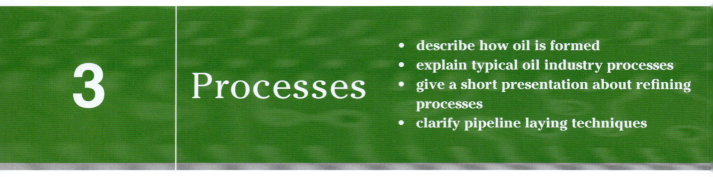

# 3 Processes

- describe how oil is formed
- explain typical oil industry processes
- give a short presentation about refining processes
- clarify pipeline laying techniques

## Exploration

Reading **1** Read this text and label the diagram with the words in the box.

| cap rock | gas | oil | reservoir rock | source rock | water |

Petroleum geologists look at two important properties of rocks: permeability and impermeability. Some rock types, such as limestone and sandstone, are highly permeable (or porous) – that is, they contain small pores (or holes) which allow fluids, such as oil, gas and water, to flow through them. Other rock types, such as granite and marble, are impermeable (or non-porous) – that is, they do not contain pores and fluids cannot pass through them. This diagram shows how permeable and impermeable rock layers are arranged in a typical oil and gas field. The oil and gas deposits are found in a layer of reservoir rock, which is permeable. In the reservoir rock, gas is at the top, oil is in the middle and water is at the bottom. The reservoir rock is trapped between two layers of impermeable rock. A long time ago, the petroleum was in a layer of source rock, such as shale, below the reservoir rock. Over a long period of time, the oil and gas flowed upwards out of the source rock into the reservoir rock, where it was trapped by the top layer of impermeable cap rock.

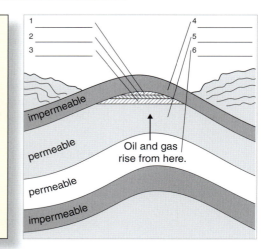

**2** Read this follow-up text and label diagrams A–C Fig 1, Fig 2 or Fig 3.

How were oil fields formed? It began millions of years ago, when the remains of microscopic plants and animals (organic matter) settled on the sea bed. Sediments, such as clay and sand, covered the organic matter. More sedimentary layers were added and the sediments became heavier. Pressure and temperature increased. The heat and pressure converted much of the organic matter into the hydrocarbons that make up oil and gas. The oil and gas then flowed upwards. Some of it reached the surface and escaped. However, some of it was trapped underground in reservoir rock below a layer of cap rock. The oil remains in this geological 'trap' until it is drilled for and brought to the surface.

Here are three types of geological trap. They were all caused by movements in the Earth's crust:

1 A fold (or anticline). The layers of rock were bent into a dome shape (see Fig 1).

2 A fault. The layers of rock cracked and one side moved upwards or downwards (see Fig 2).

3 A pinch-out. A mass of impermeable rock pushed upwards into the reservoir rock (see Fig 3).

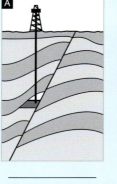
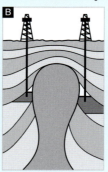
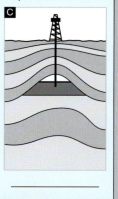

**3** Are these statements about the texts in 1 and 2 *true* (T) or *false* (F)?

1 Granite and marble are examples of reservoir rock. (T / F)
2 If there is no layer of cap rock, oil and gas can flow to the surface and escape. (T / F)
3 Oil, gas and water can flow through small holes in rocks. (T / F)
4 Oil is composed of hydrocarbons, formed underneath the sea. (T / F)

**Listening**

**4** 🔊 **10** Complete this conversation between an engineer and a visitor to a drill site with words from 1 and 2. Then listen and check your answers.

A: Can you tell me how oil fields are formed?
B: Yes, of course. It's really very simple. First, you have organic matter which falls to the sea (1) _____ .
A: Organic matter is things like plants and animals?
B: Yes, exactly. Next, this organic matter gets covered by sediments, such as clay or sand. Over time more and more sediments fall, so we end up with different sedimentary (2) _____ .
A: And the pressure increases?
B: Yes, and the (3) _____ increases too. And this process converts the organic matter into (4) _____; in other words, oil and gas.
A: I see.
B: Now this oil and gas is in what we call the source rock. After a while, it flows upwards to what we call the (5) _____ rock. And finally, it stops in a so-called (6) _____ trap.
A: Why do you call it a trap?
B: Because it can't flow upwards any more. The cap rock, which is above the reservoir and is impermeable, stops the oil and gas escaping to the surface. It traps the oil and gas.
A: I see.
B: There are different types of traps, of course. Look at these diagrams. The first one is an anticline. You can see it's shaped like a(n) (7) _____ .

**Pronunciation**

**5** 🔊 **11** Listen and repeat.

1 sedimentary layers   3 reservoir rock   5 impermeable
2 hydrocarbons        4 geological trap

**Language**

| Sequencers | |
|---|---|
| We usually use **sequencers** when we describe the different steps in a process. | *first*, *second*, *third*, *next*, *then*, *after that*, *finally* |
| We can also use certain phrases to talk about processes. | *after a while*, *over time*, *over a long period of time* |

**6** Put these sentences in the correct order. Then complete them with the words in the box.

| after   finally   first   over   then |
|---|

☐ _____, the hydrocarbons are trapped by impermeable rock or escape to the surface.
1 _____, organic matter falls to the sea bed.
☐ _____ time the hydrocarbons flow upwards.
☐ _____ that, the weight of the sedimentary layers converts the organic matter into hydrocarbons.
☐ _____, sediments fall and cover the organic matter.

# Distillation

**1** Look at this diagram of the oil distillation process. Are statements 1–6 *true* (T) or *false* (F)?

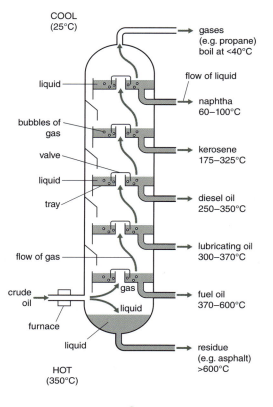

1 Crude oil is heated and pumped into the column. (T / F)
2 When this happens, all the crude oil evaporates and the vapour (or gas) rises through the column. (T / F)
3 As the vapour goes up the column, the temperature decreases. (T / F)
4 All the vapour from the crude oil flows to the top of the column and leaves it through a pipe. (T / F)
5 When the temperature falls to between 175°C and 325°C, some of the vapour condenses into liquid kerosene. (T / F)
6 This substance condenses at a higher temperature than naphtha. (T / F)

**2** Work in pairs. Read this description of the distillation process and answer the questions.

## The oil refining process: fractional distillation

Crude oil (or petroleum) is a mixture of different hydrocarbons. Many useful products can be made from them but first they must be extracted and separated from one another.

The different hydrocarbon components of crude oil are called fractions and they are separated using fractional distillation. This process is based on the principle that different substances boil at different temperatures. For example, crude oil contains kerosene (which is made into jet fuel) and naphtha (which is made into petrol for cars). When the mixture of kerosene and naphtha is heated so that it evaporates and then is cooled, the kerosene condenses at a higher temperature than the naphtha. As the mixture cools, the kerosene condenses first and the naphtha condenses later.

This is how fractional distillation works: the main equipment is a tall cylinder called a fractionator (or fractional distillation column). Inside there are many trays, or horizontal plates, located at different heights. Each tray collects a different fraction when it cools and condenses.

The crude oil is heated to at least 350°C, which makes most of the oil evaporate. The vapour then enters the column and moves up through the fractionator. As each fraction condenses, the liquid is collected in the trays. Substances with higher boiling points condense on the lower trays in the column. Substances with lower boiling points condense on the higher trays.

The trays have valves, which allow the vapour to bubble through the liquid in the tray. This helps the vapour to cool and condense more quickly. The liquid from each tray then flows out of the column.

1 Why do different substances need to be extracted from crude oil?
2 What scientific fact does fractional distillation use?
3 Which components in the column collect the condensed liquid from each fraction?
4 What do the valves do?

**3** Match 1–7 to a–g to make collocations.

| | | | |
|---|---|---|---|
| 1 | boiling | a) | oil |
| 2 | fractional | b) | cylinder |
| 3 | crude | c) | plates |
| 4 | tall | d) | fuel |
| 5 | liquid | e) | kerosene |
| 6 | horizontal | f) | distillation |
| 7 | jet | g) | point |

**4** Put these stages of the distillation process in the correct order.

☐ As the vapour rises through the trays in the column, the temperature falls.
☐ The condensed liquid of the fraction is collected in a tray.
☐ When a fraction in the vapour cools to its own boiling point, it condenses.
1 This is how the distillation process in the fractionator works.
☐ Most of the fractions in the crude oil evaporate.
☐ The condensed liquid flows out of the fractionator through a pipe from the tray.
☐ A furnace is used to heat the crude oil to a high temperature.
☐ The crude oil vapour enters the fractionator and rises up the column.

### Language

**Talking about temperature**

| We often use verb + preposition to describe **temperature changes**. | The temperature **falls to** 325°C. The temperature **rises to** between 60°C and 100°C. The temperature **ranges from** 370°C **to** 600°C. |
|---|---|

**Listening 5** 🔊 12 Complete these sentences with information from the diagram in 1. Then listen and check your answers.

1 Jet fuel is made from kerosene, which condenses between _____ and _____°C.

2 When naphtha vapour is cooled to between _____ and _____°C, it condenses.

3 Diesel oil is produced by cooling crude oil vapour to between _____ and _____°C.

4 The boiling point of industrial fuel oil ranges from _____ to _____°C.

**Speaking 6** Work in small groups. Answer these questions.

1 What is a fraction?
2 What is fractional distillation?
3 What are the main components in a fractionator?

# Refining

**Reading**    **1**    Read the text and complete this flow chart with the words in the box.

| alkylation    blending    cracking    fractional distillation    reforming    treating |

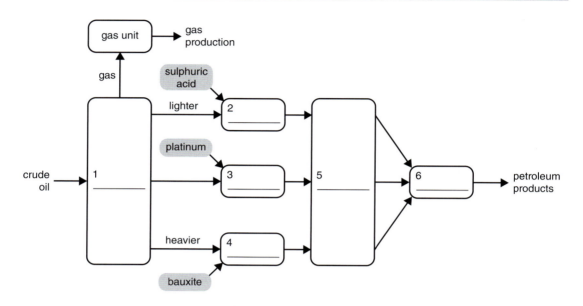

## The oil refining process: cracking, reforming, alteration, treating and blending

The molecules in petroleum are hydrocarbons and consist mainly of carbon (C) and hydrogen (H).

Hydrocarbons may be gaseous, liquid or solid at room temperature and atmospheric pressure. Solids have a higher number of carbon atoms and a higher boiling point. Gases have a lower number of carbon atoms and a lower boiling point.

After fractional distillation, petroleum fractions can be changed in three main ways: by cracking, reforming or alteration.

**Cracking** breaks down larger, heavier hydrocarbons into smaller, lighter hydrocarbons. For example, heavy gas oil can be broken down into lighter products, such as petrol and diesel. The process takes place in a cracking unit. The hydrocarbons are heated under pressure to high temperatures until they break apart (thermal cracking). Sometimes a catalyst, such as bauxite or hydrogen, is used to speed up the process.

**Reforming** combines smaller, lighter hydrocarbons to make larger, heavier

hydrocarbons. The process takes place in a reformer. It uses heat, pressure and a catalyst (usually containing platinum) to convert naphtha into high octane petrol and petrochemicals.

**Alteration** rearranges or changes the hydrocarbons in one fraction to produce a different fraction. The most common method is called alkylation, which takes place in an alkylation unit. In this process, lighter hydrocarbons are converted into high-octane petrol using a catalyst, such as sulphuric acid.

After the above processes, the fractions are treated in the treatment unit where they are passed through chemical filters to remove impurities, such as sulphur, water or salts. Finally, different fractions can be blended or mixed together in the blender to create products for making plastics and other polymers, such as petrol, lubricating oils, kerosene, jet fuel, diesel oil, heating oil and petrochemicals.

**Vocabulary**

**2** Tick ✓ which of the following are used as catalysts in the refining process.

1 ☐ kerosene     3 ☐ diesel oil     5 ☐ sulphuric acid
2 ☐ bauxite     4 ☐ water     6 ☐ platinum

**3** Match the items in this table.

| Process | Location | Purpose | Method |
|---|---|---|---|
| 1 fractional distillation | a) reformer | i) remove sulphur | A) heat under high pressure |
| 2 cracking | b) blender | ii) break down heavy hydrocarbons | B) cool fractions at different temperatures |
| 3 reforming | c) alkylation unit | iii) separate fractions from crude oil | C) heat under pressure; use platinum as catalyst |
| 4 alkylation | d) treatment unit | iv) create products, such as petrol | D) use sulphuric acid as catalyst |
| 5 treating | e) distillation column | v) change hydrocarbons | E) mix fractions together |
| 6 blending | f) cracking unit | vi) combine hydrocarbons | F) pass through chemical filters |

**Listening**

**4** ▶ 🎧 13 Complete these sentences from a presentation about the refining process with the words and phrases in the box. Then put the sentences in the correct order. Then listen and check your answers.

> brings me to   by saying   for coming   let's look at
> like to   move   shown   shows   to explain   turn to

☐ (1) _____ cracking first.
☐ That (2) _____ the three main processes: cracking, reforming and alteration.
☐ My objective in this talk is (3) _____ some of the processes in oil refining.
☐ As (4) _____ in the flow chart, after treatment we have blending.
☐ I'd like to start (5) _____ a few things about hydrocarbons.
☐ Now let's (6) _____ on to reforming.
☐ And thirdly, let's (7) _____ alteration.
☐ And finally, I'd (8) _____ mention some of the products of refining.
☐ As the flow chart (9) _____, the next process is treatment.
☐1 Good morning everyone, and thanks (10) _____ to this presentation.

**Language**

**The passive with *can***

We use *can + be* + past participle to form the passive with *can*.

| Active | Passive |
|---|---|
| We **can change** fractions in three main ways. | Fractions **can be changed** in three main ways. |
| We **can break** large hydrocarbons **down** into smaller ones. | Large hydrocarbons **can be broken down** into smaller ones. |

**5** Read the text in 1 again. Underline the passives with *can*.

**Speaking**

**6** Work in small groups. Prepare a short presentation on the refining process. Use the expressions in 4 to help you. Then give a presentation to your group.

# Laying a pipeline

**Reading**  **1** Read the text and match headings 1–7 to gaps a–g.

1 Burying the pipeline under the sea bed
2 Connecting the pipes into a pipeline
3 Laying the pipeline on the sea bed
4 Surveying and mapping the sea bed
5 Cleaning out the pipeline before use
6 Constructing the pipes
7 Planning the route of the pipeline

Most offshore oil and gas is brought to shore by pipelines, which can operate in all weathers. Here are the main stages of laying a sub-sea pipeline:

a) ___ The sea bed is mapped to identify unstable areas and obstacles and to see if it will be possible to bury the pipe.

b) ___ Pipeline routes are planned to be as short as possible. Slopes that could put stress on unsupported pipe are avoided.

c) ___ Pipeline construction is begun onshore. Lengths of pipe are waterproofed with bitumen and coated with polymers or steel-reinforced concrete. This coating protects the submarine pipeline and also weighs it down on the sea bed.

d) ___ The prepared lengths of pipe are welded together offshore on a lay barge.

e) ___ The barge is winched forward on its anchor lines. At the same time, the pipeline drops gently to the sea bed. The pipeline is guided by a 'stinger'.

f) ___ Two methods are often used to cover and protect the pipeline on the sea bed:

1 (see Fig 1 in 2) In shallower water, a pipe-trenching barge is used. This vessel follows the lay barge. When the new pipeline is laid on the sea bed, the trenching barge digs a shallow trench under the pipeline and covers it with debris.

2 (see Fig 2 in 2) In deeper water, a gravel-dumping vessel is used. This vessel follows the semi-submersible lay barge and drops gravel onto the pipeline. The pipeline has more weight in deeper seas.

g) ___ The insides of pipelines are cleaned regularly to remove wax deposits and water. A pipeline inspection gauge is forced through the pipe. This device collects deposits and cleans the pipe.

**2** Look at methods 1 and 2 in the text in 1. Label these diagrams Fig 1 or Fig 2. Then label the diagrams with the words in the box. Use four of the words twice.

anchor   anchor line   gravel   pipeline   stinger   trench

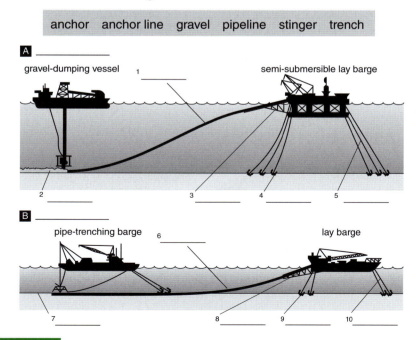

A _____
gravel-dumping vessel    1 _____    semi-submersible lay barge
2 _____    3 _____  4 _____   5 _____

B _____
pipe-trenching barge   6 _____    lay barge
7 _____    8 _____  9 _____   10 _____

**3** Match 1–8 to a–h to make sentences.

| | | | |
|---|---|---|---|
| 1 | Routes | a) | are dug. |
| 2 | The sea bed | b) | are planned. |
| 3 | Slopes | c) | are avoided. |
| 4 | Pipes | d) | is dropped. |
| 5 | The barge | e) | are cleaned. |
| 6 | Trenches | f) | is mapped. |
| 7 | Gravel | g) | are welded. |
| 8 | The insides | h) | is winched forward. |

**Listening** **4** 🌀 **14** Listen to three conversations about laying pipelines. What mistakes do the speakers make?

1 She says _____ instead of _____ .
2 He says _____ instead of _____ .
3 She says _____ instead of _____ .

**5** Listen again and answer these questions.

1 What words and phrases do the speakers use to correct themselves?
2 What do the speakers say to point out the mistakes?

**Language**

---

**Correcting**

| | |
|---|---|
| We use certain expressions to **correct** ourselves when we make mistakes. | **Oh sorry, my mistake.** Onshore, not offshore.<br>**I mean/I meant** shallow water, not deep water.<br>**I got that wrong. I meant** the pipeline. |
| We can correct other people by repeating the word we think is wrong or by asking for clarification. | **Did I understand you correctly?** You use trenches in deep water?<br>**Do you mean** 'offshore'?<br>**So in other words,** the stinger places the gravel in the right place? |

---

**6** Read these conversations about laying pipelines and complete them with suitable expressions. Use language from the Language box.

1
A: Yes, so we try to make the pipeline routes as long as possible.
B: As long as possible?
A: _____

2
A: We have a team of engineers on the lay barge. Their job is to weld the pipes together.
B: Do you mean 'welders'?
A: _____

3
A: We use a pipeline inspection gauge to clean the outside of the pipe.
B: Sorry, did you say the outside?
A: _____

**Speaking** **7** Work in pairs. Student A, explain how pipes are laid underwater but make some mistakes. Student B, correct Student A or ask for clarification where necessary.

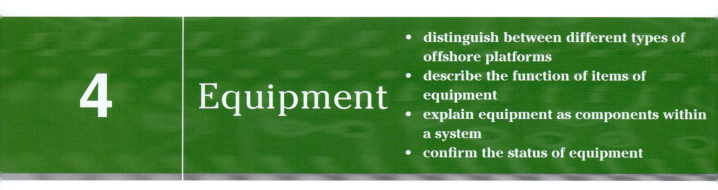

# 4   Equipment

- **distinguish between different types of offshore platforms**
- **describe the function of items of equipment**
- **explain equipment as components within a system**
- **confirm the status of equipment**

## Types of rigs

**Reading**   **1**   Read the text and match these types of offshore oil platform (A–E) to gaps 1–5.

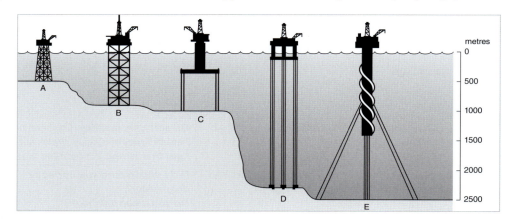

# Types of offshore oil platform

Offshore oil platforms must be strong enough to resist wind speeds of over 150 km per hour and waves over 20 m high.

(1) ___ Spar platforms are the largest type of offshore platform. They are mounted on a large cylinder. This is attached to the sea bed by cables and lines. The cylinder stabilises the platform in the water and allows it to move a little during storms. Spar platforms can operate in water from about 700 m to over 3,000 m deep.

(2) ___ Tension leg platforms do not have a cylinder. The platform is mounted on long, flexible legs. These go down from the platform to the sea bed. They allow the platform to move from side to side in a storm but not up and down. Tension leg platforms can operate in water up to about 2,300 m deep.

(3) ___ Fixed platforms are attached to the sea bed with rigid legs. The legs are fixed to the sea bed with piles. They are stable and resist wind and water forces. Fixed platforms can operate in water depths up to about 500 m.

(4) ___ Compliant towers are like fixed platforms. The platform is mounted on a narrow, flexible tower. The tower extends from the platform to a solid foundation on the sea bed. It is flexible, and this allows the platform to operate in much deeper water, between 450 m and 900 m.

(5) ___ Sea star platforms are similar to tension leg platforms but smaller. The platform floats on a short cylinder and a hull. The cylinder and hull are below sea level, and the hull is filled with water. The hull is attached to tension legs. These narrow, flexible legs extend from the hull to the sea bed. The platform can move a little from side to side but not up and down. It can operate in water depths of up to about 1,000 m.

**Writing**   **2**   Write short notes about the most important features of each type of offshore oil platform in 1. Use the information in the text in 1 to help you.

*Spar platforms: largest, cylinder, cables and lines, 700–3,000 m*

**Listening** **3** ▶ 🔘 **15** Listen to six statements about different types of offshore oil platform. Are the statements *true* (T) or *false* (F)?

1  (T / F)   2  (T / F)   3  (T / F)   4  (T / F)   5  (T / F)   6  (T / F)

**Language** **4** Complete these sentences with the correct form of the adjectives in brackets. Use *more*, *the most*, *less* or *the least* if necessary.

1  The cylinder on the spar is _____ (long) and _____ (wide) than the one on the sea star.
2  Oil companies use spar platforms in _____ (deep) waters in the world.
3  The ocean is too _____ (deep) for the fixed platform or the compliant tower.
4  The spar is _____ (strong) and _____ (flexible) of all the platforms.
5  The fixed platform is _____ (flexible) of all the platforms.
6  The spar platform is too _____ (long) for the shallow waters near the coast.

---

### Modifying comparisons

| | |
|---|---|
| We can make comparisons stronger or weaker by using modifiers before the adjective. To make them stronger, we can use **a lot**, **much** or **far**. To make them weaker, we can use **a little**, **a bit** or **slightly**. | Spar platforms go **much deeper** than fixed platforms. <br> Fixed platforms are **slightly smaller** than compliant platforms. |

---

**5** Complete this article with the correct form of the words in brackets and appropriate modifiers.

# The minimum facilities platform (MFP)

The MFP is a small platform with no permanent crew and remote operation. It is (1) _____ (light) than the spar and operates in (2) _____ (shallow) waters. The legs of the MFP are (3) _____ (short) and are (4) _____ (cheap) to build than the cylinder of the spar. All the MFP wellheads are on the platform, while the spar wellheads are sub-sea. This means that oil production on the MFP is (5) _____ (easy) than on the spar. However, it has (6) _____ (few) wellheads and produces (7) _____ (little) oil than the spar. A maximum of 12 crew members can stay on the MFP platform. The spar platform is one of the (8) _____ (large) platforms in the world and can operate in the (9) _____ (deep) waters in the world. On the other hand, the MFP is one of the (10) _____ (economical) platforms in the world.

| | Minimum facilities platform (MFP) | Spar platform |
|---|---|---|
| 1  Depth of water | 15–100 m | 700–3,000 m |
| 2  Capacity | 15,000 bpd* | 55,000 bpd |
| 3  Weight of deck | 1,000 tons | 17,000 tons |
| 4  Number of wellheads | 6 | 20 |
| 5  Crew capacity | 12 | 110 |
| 6  Length of support | legs: 15–100 m (same as sea) | cylinder: 230 m cables: 1,000 m |

*bpd = barrels per day

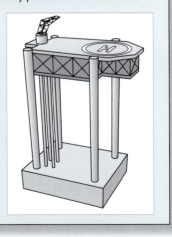

**Writing** **6** Rewrite the article in 5 so that the spar platform is the focus. Start like this: *The spar is much heavier than the MFP and operates in much deeper waters … .*

# The blowout preventer

Listening

**1**  ▶ 🔵 **16**  Listen to this speaker. What is a blowout?

**2**  Listen again. Label this diagram with the words in the box.

BOP = blowout preventer

> annular BOP   blind ram BOP   shear ram BOP

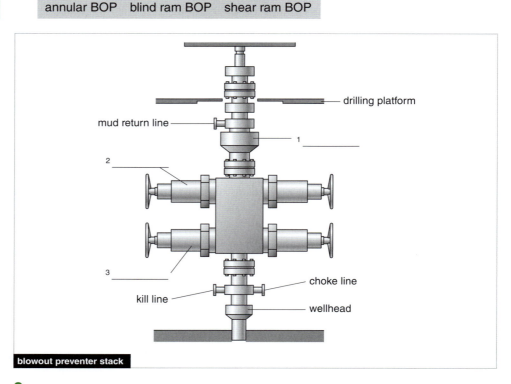

mud return line

drilling platform

1

2

3

kill line

choke line

wellhead

**blowout preventer stack**

Reading

**3**  Read the article about BOPs and match diagrams A–C to gaps 1–3.

A

B   drill pipe

C   drill pipe

The annular BOP (1) (___) forms a seal in the annular space (or annulus) between the drill pipe and the casing of the well bore. In this type of valve, the seal is made of elastomer (or elastic polymer) and is ring-shaped. The seal is mechanically squeezed inwards to close the annulus. The blind ram BOP (2) (___) has two steel plates which move together like gates and seal the complete well hole. The sealing surfaces of the steel plates have elastomer components. Blind rams cannot be used when there is a drill string in the well hole. In this situation, either the annular BOP or the shear rams are used. Shear rams (3) (___) have two steel blades which move together and close the well hole by cutting through the drill pipe. The section of drill pipe is destroyed but the rest of the drill string is unharmed by the shear rams.

When the well hole or annulus is completely closed, the drillers begin the kill operation. This procedure is designed to stop the well from flowing. High-density drilling mud is pumped into the well through the kill line (or pipe). The mud weighs down the fluid from the well through force of gravity and controls the flow. Then the mud leaves the well hole via the choke line. The kill line and the choke line are small-diameter pipes.

**Language**

**4**   Match questions 1–6 to answers a–f.

1   What's the BOP for?
2   Where is the BOP located?
3   Why is the BOP needed?
4   How is the well shut down by the blind ram BOP?
5   When do the oil workers start the kill procedure?
6   How are the rams on the BOP operated?

a)  It's located at the top of the well hole, between the drilling platform and the ground.
b)  By means of powerful hydraulic pistons.
c)  It's for shutting down a well during a blowout and for preventing fluids from escaping.
d)  It's done by sliding together two heavy steel plates and sealing the well hole.
e)  They start the kill procedure after the BOP has completely sealed the well hole.
f)  It's needed to protect the oil workers, the drilling equipment and the environment during a blowout.

**5**   Use the information in 3 to name the items described in these sentences.

1   This device is for controlling the flow of fluids under high pressure from a well hole. _____
2   This device prevents fluids from flowing through the space between the drill pipe and the casing of the well bore. _____
3   This device closes a well hole which contains a drill string. It does this by shearing through the drill pipe. _____
4   This is a narrow pipe which carries heavy drilling mud out of the blowout preventer. _____
5   This device is made of a polymer with good elasticity and is shaped like a ring. _____
6   These two components look like a pair of heavy shears. _____
7   These two parts are in the shape of heavy steel doors or gates, which slide together. _____

**Speaking**   **6**   Work in pairs. Student A, look at the information on page 68. Student B, look at the information on page 76. Follow the instructions.

# The circulation system

**1** Label 1–6 in this diagram with the words in the box.

casing   drill bit   drill collar   drill string   kelly   swivel

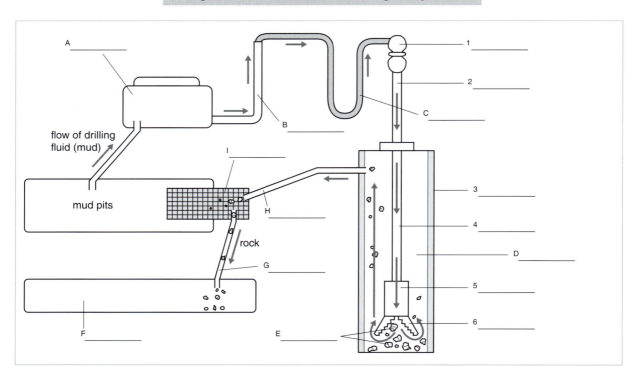

Reading **2** Read this text and label A–I in the diagram in 1 with the words in **bold**.

## The circulation system

The circulation system cleans out the well. It pumps a special liquid (called drilling fluid or drilling mud) down the drill string into the well hole. This liquid picks up pieces of rock (**rock cuttings**) and carries them up the well hole and out of the well.

This is how the system works: the **mud pump** sucks the drilling fluid from large open tanks (called mud pits) and pumps it through the **stand pipe** and the **rotary hose**. The fluid then enters the kelly through a hole in the swivel. It then moves through the kelly and the drill string to the drill bit.

Then the mud flows out of the drill bit and around the bottom of the well. It collects the rock cuttings and carries them up through the **annulus** (the space between the drill string and the casing). At the top of the annulus, the mud and cuttings leave the well through the **mud return line** (or pipe).

Next, the mud flows into the **shaker**. This moves quickly from side to side. The fluid flows through the small holes in the shaker but the large rock cuttings stay on the shaker. The fluid then flows back into the mud pits and the large cuttings slide down the **shale slide** into the **reserve pit**.

**3** Match 1–5 to a–e to make collocations.

1 circulation
2 rock
3 drill
4 shale
5 stand

a) cuttings
b) string
c) pipe
d) system
e) slide

**Vocabulary** **4** Choose the correct words in *italics*.

1 The mud enters the swivel through an *inlet / outlet* in the swivel.
2 The mud leaves the drill bit through an *inlet / outlet* in the bit.
3 The rotary hose connects the *pump / drill bit* to the rotary equipment.
4 The mud flows *into / out of* the well through the drill string.

**Language**

**Prepositions of movement**

| | |
|---|---|
| We use **prepositions of movement**, (e.g. *down*, *through*, *around*) to describe how things move through a system. | *The mud leaves* **through** *the outlet pipe.*<br>*The mud flows* **around** *the bottom of the well.* |

**5** Complete this text about the circulation system with the prepositions in the box.

around   down   from   into   out of   through   up (x2)

This is how the drilling mud flows (1) _____ the whole circulation system. The pump sucks the mud (2) _____ the mud pits. The pump then pushes the mud (3) _____ the stand pipe and (4) _____ the rotary hose (5) _____ the swivel. Next, it flows (6) _____ the kelly and the drill string. Then the mud comes (7) _____ the drill bit and enters the well hole. Finally, the fluid collects the cuttings and flows back (8) _____ the well hole.

**Listening** **6** 🔊 **17** Put these circulation system stages in the correct order. Then listen and check your answers.

☐ It then flows down through the drill string.
☐ From the rotary hose, the fluid enters the swivel and the kelly.
☐ 1 The pumps suck the drilling mud out of the mud pits.
☐ Then it leaves the drill bit and flows around the annulus.
☐ The fluid picks up pieces of rock and sand.
☐ The fluid then goes into the mud pits again and the cuttings enter the reserve pit.
☐ The shaker takes the cuttings out of the fluid.
☐ At the top of the well, the fluid flows through the mud return line into the shaker.
☐ Then the mud rises up the well hole between the drill pipe and the casing.
☐ They then pump the fluid through a hose to the rotary equipment.

**Vocabulary** **7** Complete these sentences with the correct form of one of the verbs in brackets.

1 The pumps _____ (push/pull) drilling mud out of the mud pits and _____ (push/pull) it through the rotary hose.
2 The rotary hose _____ (carry/flow) the drilling mud into the swivel.
3 The mud _____ (pass/leave) into the kelly through a hole in the swivel and then _____ (flow/contain) through the drill string.
4 The drilling mud _____ (enter/leave) the well hole through the mud return line.
5 In the shaker, the mud _____ (rise/sink) through the holes but the rock cuttings _____ (stay/flow) on the shaker.

**Speaking** **8** Work in pairs. Take turns to explain how a circulation system works on an oil rig. Use the diagram in 1 to help you.

# Pipeline components

**1** Read the text and label this diagram with the words in the box.

| control station | gauges | pipeline | regulator station | supply station | terminal |

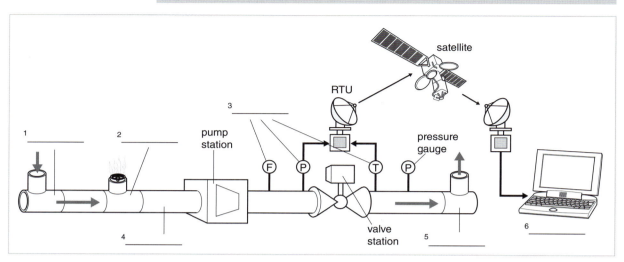

## Components of oil and gas pipelines

Pipeline: This is normally made of steel and covered with a moisture-resistant material. It carries gas or oil from a supply station to a terminal.

Supply station: This injects the product (oil or gas) into the pipeline.

Pump station (for oil) or compressor station (for gas): These push the product along the pipeline.

Valve station: The operator can close two valve stations and isolate the pipeline between them. Then he can do maintenance work or isolate a break or leak in the pipe. Valve stations are usually located every 10–30 km along the line.

Regulator station: The operator can release pressure from the pipeline here.

Terminal: The product leaves the pipeline here.

There are three measuring instruments: flow gauges (F) measure the speed of product along the pipeline; pressure gauges (P) measure pressure; temperature gauges (T) measure temperature.

The remote terminal unit (RTU) receives the information from the three gauges and sends it to the control station by satellite or mobile phone link.

The control station contains computers. They receive all the data from the RTUs and check for leaks. The computer operator can open or close valves and control compressors or pumps.

**Vocabulary** **2** Match the pipeline components 1–6 to their functions a–f.

1 The pipeline
2 The valve station
3 The supply station
4 The regulator station
5 The terminal
6 The gauges

a) measure heat, pressure and flow along the pipeline.
b) is the outlet for the whole pipeline.
c) transports oil or gas from one place to another.
d) lowers the pressure in the pipeline.
e) is the inlet for the whole pipeline.
f) can stop the flow of oil or gas.

**3** Complete these sentences with the correct form of the verbs in the box.

> check   compress   fall   give   measure
> pump   receive   send   switch off   transmit

1 The purpose of the flow gauge is to _____ the speed of the oil along the pipeline.
2 The compressor station _____ the gas and _____ it under pressure along the line.
3 One function of the control station computers is to _____ valve stations and to _____ compressors if there is a leak.
4 One function of the temperature gauge is to _____ a warning if the heat is rising.
5 If there is a leak in the pipeline and the pressure _____, the pressure valve _____ this information through the RTU to the control station.
6 The job of the RTU is to _____ information from the gauges and _____ it to the control station.

Listening **4** ▶ 🔊 **18** Listen to a conversation between two men. Where are they?

**5** Listen again and answer these questions.
1 What is Kevin's problem?
2 What is Rob's problem?
3 What is the plan?

**Language**

### Contractions

| In spoken English we often use **contractions** in negative structures. | will not → won't | have not → haven't |
| --- | --- | --- |
| | has not → hasn't | is not → isn't |
| | do not → don't | did not → didn't |
| | are not → aren't/'re not | cannot → can't |

**6** Answer these questions. Use contractions where possible.
1 'Are the valve stations open?' 'Yes, _____ .'
2 'Will the operators open the valves if there is a leak?' 'No, _____ .'
3 'Have they checked the temperature gauges yet?' 'No, _____ .'
4 'Is the compressor switched off?' 'No, _____ .'
5 'Did the pressure gauges indicate a rise in pressure?' 'No, _____ .'
6 'Has the computer received all the data from the RTUs?' 'Yes, _____ .'

**Speaking** **7** Work in pairs. Student A, look at the information on this page. Student B, look at the information on page 76. Follow the instructions.

**Student A**
You are a line walker inspecting a pipeline. Listen to track 18 again and roleplay a similar conversation with Student B, an engineer at the control station.

# 5 Project management

- discuss progress on an oil rig project
- explain plans during project meetings
- outline alternatives
- present an idea

## In a meeting

Reading **1** It is the fourth week of February in an oil rig project. Read the schedule and answer these questions.

excavate = dig

1 Have they excavated the reserve pit yet?
2 When did they transport the equipment to the rig location?
3 What are they doing now?
4 When will they put the kelly into position?

### Preparing the site and the rig before drilling

| Task | January | | | | February | | | | March | | | |
|------|---------|---|---|---|----------|---|---|---|-------|---|---|---|
| Week | 1 | 2 | 3 | 4 | 1 | 2 | 3 | 4 | 1 | 2 | 3 | 4 |
| level site (use bulldozers) | ■ | | | | | | | | | | | |
| dig mud and reserve pits | | ■ | | | | | | | | | | |
| drill starter hole and mouse hole | | | ■ | | | | | | | | | |
| transport equipment to rig location | | | | ■ | | | | | | | | |
| install power system | | | | | ■ | | | | | | | |
| assemble rig platform | | | | | | ■ | | | | | | |
| raise derrick on platform | | | | | | | ■ | | | | | |
| install lifting and rotary system | | | | | | | | ■ | ■ | | | |
| set up mud tanks and mud pumps | | | | | | | | ■ | ■ | | | |
| connect mud pipes and hoses | | | | | | | | ■ | ■ | | | |
| string electrical cables | | | | | | | | | | ■ | | |
| put kelly into position on block | | | | | | | | | | | ■ | |
| set up pipe racks and drill pipes | | | | | | | | | | | | ■ |

**2** Complete this conversation with the correct form of verbs from the table in 1.

A: Hello, Hamish. How are you getting on? (1) _____ the derrick on the platform yet?

B: Yes, we have.

A: Great. When (2) _____ the rig platform?

B: Let's see. Yes, we (3) _____ it in the first week of February.

A: So (4) _____ the lifting and rotary system now?

B: Yes, we are.

A: What else are you doing now?

B: We (5) _____ the tanks and pumps, and (6) _____ the pipes and hoses.

A: OK. That's good. When (7) _____ the electrical cables?

B: We'll do that in the second week of March.

Listening **3**  ▶ 🔊 19  Listen and check your answers in 2.

**Language**

### Past simple and present perfect

| | |
|---|---|
| We use the **past simple** to talk about a completed action in the past. | When **did** you **assemble** the rig platform?<br>We **assembled** it last week/in the first week of March. |
| We use the **present perfect** (*have* + past participle) to talk about things that happened in the past but not at a specific time. | I **have discussed** this with the drilling engineer.<br>They **haven't installed** the lifting system.<br>**Have** you **raised** the derrick yet?<br>Who **has** he **spoken** to? |

4 Complete this progress report about the project in 1 with the correct past simple or present perfect form of the verbs in the box.

> assemble   dig   drill   install   not assemble
> not install   not string   raise   transport

The team have levelled the site with bulldozers. They (1) _____ the mud and reserve pits, and they (2) _____ the starter hole and the mouse hole. During the fourth week of January they (3) _____ the equipment to the rig location. They (4) _____ the power system at the end of January but they (5) _____ the rig platform then. They (6) _____ it in the first week of February.

The crew (7) _____ the derrick on the platform but they (8) _____ the lifting and rotary systems yet. Another crew are setting up the mud tanks and the mud pumps, and a third crew are connecting the mud pipes and hoses. They (9) _____ the electric cables yet. According to the schedule, they'll put the cables in in the second week of March and they'll put the kelly into position during the third week of March.

5 Complete these conversations about the project in 1.

1 A: Have you seen the company representative?
B: Yes, I've just _____ him.

2 A: Have you been to the rig?
B: No, I _____ .

3 A: Has the toolpusher arrived yet?
B: Yes, he _____ . He's in Building 13.

4 A: Why haven't you strung the electric cables?
B: We've _____ busy with the mud pumps.

5 A: Have they finished?
B: Not yet. They've _____ the mud tanks and pumps but they haven't _____ the pipes and hoses.

**Speaking**  6 Work in pairs. Read this list of tasks for dismantling the rig and put the tasks in the best order.

☐ Detach the kelly from the travelling block.
☐ Fill in the mud and reserve pits.
☐ Disconnect the mud pipes and hoses from the equipment.
☐ Dismantle the rig platform.
☐ Take down all the electric cables.
☐ Lower the derrick.
☐ Remove the equipment from the site.
☐ Uninstall the power system.

7 Work in pairs. Student A, look at the information on page 68. Student B, look at the information on page 76. Follow the instructions.

# Plans

**Listening**   **1**    **20**   Listen to three managers in meetings with their teams and match conversations 1–3 to photos A–C.

**2**   Listen again and answer these questions.

**Conversation 1**

1 Why can't they use the helicopters?
2 When will the bus be there?
3 How long will the journey take?
4 Will it be dark when they arrive?

**Conversation 2**

5 Why are they having the meeting?
6 Who is the project from?
7 What has been in short supply?
8 When must the report be ready?

**Conversation 3**

9 What are they supplying?
10 How many ships are involved?
11 When is Harry flying out?
12 What is on the way?

**Vocabulary**   **3**   Read audio script 20 on page 72. What do the underlined words and phrases in these sentences mean?

1 The bus will be here in about an hour, so you all have time to <u>grab</u> a cup of coffee.
   a) make        b) drink       c) buy

2 And then the boat will take another six or seven hours <u>on top of that</u>.
   a) in addition      b) in total       c) at the most

3 I'll <u>amend</u> the schedule on the bus.
   a) change        b) write up     c) delete

4 <u>Diesel oil has been in very short supply</u>, for example.
   a) Diesel oil has been delivered quickly.
   b) There is too much diesel oil.
   c) There hasn't been enough diesel oil.

5 So this office will be visiting all refineries in the country to check exactly what is happening <u>on the ground</u>.
   a) on the surface of the ground     b) in the earth     c) in the place where things are happening

6 Four packages. Must <u>be worth a bit</u>.
   a) need a lot of time     b) cost a good amount of money     c) not cost much money

**4**   Match 1–8 to a–h to make sentences.

1 You all have time to grab                a) on the ground.
2 It'll be dark                           b) a bit.
3 This project comes straight from      c) to normal.
4 Diesel oil has been in very        d) when we get there.
5 We need to check exactly what is happening    e) short supply.
6 After that it's back                f) on the agenda.
7 This is the next item             g) the minister.
8 That must be worth             h) a cup of coffee.

**Language**

**Future forms**

We use different forms to talk about the future.

| | |
|---|---|
| *be + going to* + infinitive | It's **going to be** a long day. |
| *will* (*'ll*) | I**'ll amend** the schedule on the bus. |
| Present continuous (*be + -ing*) | We**'re starting** deliveries next month. |
| Future continuous (*will + be + -ing*) | I**'ll be leaving** at eight tomorrow morning. |
| It is often possible to use different forms without any major change in meaning. | We**'re going to start** deliveries next month. <br> We**'ll start** deliveries next month. <br> We**'re starting** deliveries next month. <br> We**'ll be starting** deliveries next month. |

**5** Read audio script 20 on page 72 and underline all the future forms.

**6** Match questions 1–6 to answers a–i. For some questions, more than one answer is possible.

1. So what's happening?
2. What are you doing?
3. Where's John going?
4. How are you getting there?
5. When will you let me know?
6. What are they going to do?

a) We'll be working on the Brazil project.
b) I'm going by bus.
c) We're meeting at three.
d) We're going to leave early.
e) I'll confirm tomorrow by email.
f) We're working on the Brazil project.
g) We're going to work on the Brazil project.
h) They're going to repair the pump.
i) To the office. He's coming straight back, don't worry.

**Writing**

**7** What will you be doing in 15 years' time? Complete these sentences. Then add two more.

1. In 15 years' time I will probably be working for _____ .
2. I will be living in _____ .
3. I will have _____ .
4. I won't have _____ .
5. I won't be _____ .

**Speaking**

**8** Work in pairs. Look at these situations. Take turns to explain what you will do. You must give different solutions.

1. You work on a rig. You need to speak to the toolpusher but he is in a meeting.
2. You want to visit a new country but it's very expensive.
3. You would like to practise your English but your lessons are too short.
4. Your car has broken down.
5. You work in a refinery. You see smoke coming from a road tanker.
6. You want to transfer some files to your USB stick but it's full.
7. The photocopier is jammed.

A: *I'll come back later.*
B: *I'll try calling him on the phone.*

**9** Work in pairs. Discuss your plans for next week/month/year.

# Alternative solutions

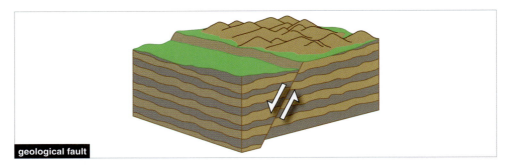

geological fault

**Listening** **1** ▶ 🎵 **21** Listen to a project manager talking about a new pipeline. What is the problem with the original route? What are the alternatives?

**2** Listen again. What are the issues relating to the different alternatives?

**3** ▶ 🎵 **22** Listen to a telephone conversation. What three types of water bodies are mentioned?

**4** Listen again. What is the good news?

**Vocabulary** **5** Different methods for crossing or diverting water are mentioned in the telephone conversation in 3. List as many as you can. Then read audio script 22 on pages 72–73 to check your answers.

**6** Match 1–4 to illustrations A–D.

1 Open cut: a trench is dug through the minor waterway (also known as a wet ditch).
2 Flume: the flow of the river is diverted through a pipe.
3 Dam and pump: the river is blocked and the water is pumped past the excavation area.
4 Horizontal directional drilling: a hole is drilled underneath the river and the pipe is passed through.

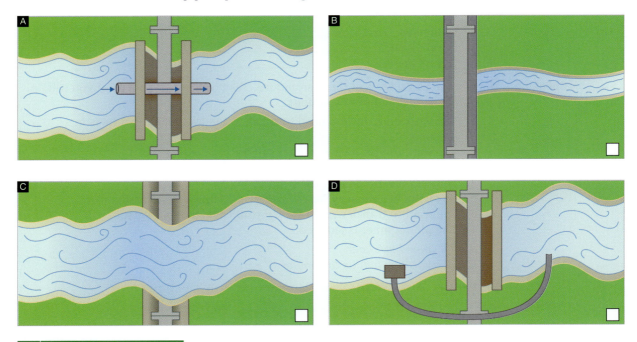

**Language**

<table>
<tr><td colspan="2">First conditional</td></tr>
<tr>
<td>We use the first conditional to talk about a situation and a possible result in the future. We use: if + present tense, will + infinitive. When the sentence starts with if, we put a comma after the if clause.</td>
<td>If we choose the wetlands route, we will need temporary accommodation for the workers./We will need temporary accommodation for the workers if we choose the wetlands route. If we use existing pipelines, we will have to increase capacity./ We will have to increase capacity if we use existing pipelines.</td>
</tr>
</table>

**7** Complete these sentences from the conversations in 1 and 3. Then listen to tracks 21 and 22 again and check your answers.

1  If I _____ my team on it today, you _____ something on your desk by, say, next Monday.
2  If we _____ a pipeline there, we _____ build access roads and housing for the workers.
3  If we _____ to cross intermediate water bodies, we _____ divert the water.
4  If we _____ in the dry season, we _____ to use open-cut methods.
5  If there _____ no water flow, we _____ to use open cut.
6  So if we _____ things right, we _____ a lot of money.

**8** Complete this conversation with sentences a–e.

Ali:     If we take the bus, we'll be there by nightfall.
Salim: (1) ____
Ali:     It will be cheaper if we take the bus. And it's my budget we're using. The helicopter is too expensive.
Salim: (2) ____
Ali:     Not my problem.
Salim: (3) ____
Ali:     OK, OK. You win. Let's take the helicopter then.
Salim: (4) ____
Ali:     What's that?
Salim: (5) ____
Ali:     Now wait a minute …

a)  And then he'll kill you. Because I will tell him if you insist on the bus.
b)  I'll take the helicopter and you take the bus. If we do that, we will both be happy.
c)  On the other hand, if we take the helicopter, we will be there by lunchtime.
d)  There is one other option.
e)  True, very true. But I do have a meeting in the afternoon. If I miss that, the boss will kill me.

**9** Complete these sentences so they are true for you.

1  If I win the lottery, I will …
2  If I get promoted, I will …
3  If I lose my watch, I will …
4  If my company asks me to move to a new location, I will …

**Speaking 10** Work in pairs. Roleplay the conversation in 8. Practise reading the conversation a few times and change your intonation each time until you are happy with the result. Then act out the conversation without the book.

# Presenting your idea

**Speaking** **1** Work in pairs. Match 1–3 to photos A–C. What happens at each of these places?

1 bunded storage tanks  2 tanker jetty  3 customer collection facility

**Listening** **2** 🎧 **23** Listen to a project manager explaining a project. List the three elements the scope of the project consists of. What does *scope* mean?

DWT = deadweight ton

**3** Listen again and complete these sentences.

1 The new jetty will handle tankers of up to _____ .
2 The expansion of the fuel storage facility will include a new customer _____ .
3 The storage facility will have a capacity of _____ .
4 The facility will be able to store seven different _____ .
5 The new pipeline system will follow the old _____ .

**4** Match questions 1–5 to answers a–e.

1 What does *bunded* mean?
2 Will the new storage tanks be above ground or underground?
3 Can you tell us more about the customer collection facility?
4 What about new buildings?
5 You mentioned a new storage capacity of 89,000m³. Will this be enough?

a) Currently we are looking at both options.
b) Yes. Basically, we are looking at rail loading and road loading. The annual throughput capacity will be in the region of 600,000 m³ per year.
c) It means that the tank is enclosed within a secondary containment system, such as a wall, to contain any liquids that escape from the tank.
d) Actually, I think I said that the new capacity was 189,000m³. And yes, we think that it will be enough.
e) The main constructions will be the bund areas, two new buildings, one for offices and one for technical facilities such as workshops, control room, generator room and so on, and the new roads and railway lines.

**Vocabulary** **5** Choose the correct words in *italics*.

1 storage *customer / facility / tanker*
2 tanker *storage / works / jetty*
3 bund *area / tanker / workshop*
4 containment *throughput / loading / system*
5 product *facility / type / road*
6 rail *loading / room / building*
7 annual *collection / construction / throughput*

**Language**

## Adverbs

Some **adverbs** express how the speaker feels about something. They can be used at the beginning or end of sentences, as well as in front of the main verb.

| |
|---|
| The new pipeline will **hopefully** follow the same route as the old one. (*hopefully* = I hope) |
| **Basically**, the new jetty will be able to handle tankers of up to 50,000 DWT instead of 12,000. (*basically* = this is the most important information) |
| I can **honestly** say that was the best presentation I have ever seen. (*honestly* = in truth) |
| I think I said 189,000m³, **actually**. (*actually* = in fact) |
| **Obviously**, we couldn't work in the dark, so we all went home. (*obviously* = this can easily be seen or understood) |

---

apparently = I have heard
fortunately = luckily
personally = from my point of view
really = in truth, in reality

**6** Complete these sentences with the adverbs in the box.

> apparently   fortunately   hopefully   personally   really

1  I have just been speaking to Gerald. _____, the government wants to build a new refinery outside the town but I don't _____ believe it. Do you?
2  _____, we'll start work next week but it depends on the weather.
3  There was a fire last night in one of the bunded tanks. _____, it didn't spread.
4  _____ I have never been on an oil rig but I hope to go one day.

**Speaking**  **7** Work in pairs. Student A, look at the information on this page. Student B, look at the information on page 77. Follow the instructions.

**Vancouver International Airport** will be holding a press conference tomorrow to present their plans for a new aviation fuel delivery system. The press conference will take place in Terminal 1 and will start at 10 a.m. Members of the public are welcome.

**Student A**
1  Read this newspaper ad. What is it about? Discuss with Student B.
2  Look at this photo of the proposed aviation fuel delivery system to serve the airlines at Vancouver International Airport. Label the photo. Then describe the layout to Student B.

# 6 Products

- talk about properties of oil
- discuss underground storage facilities
- explain pipeline contamination control
- follow hazmat transportation regulations

## Oils

**Reading** **1** Read the text and label illustrations A–H with the adjectives in the box.

> flammable  fluid  immiscible  miscible
> non-flammable  stable  viscous  volatile

| A | B | C | D |
|---|---|---|---|
| | | oil / water | salt / water |

| E | F | G | H |
|---|---|---|---|

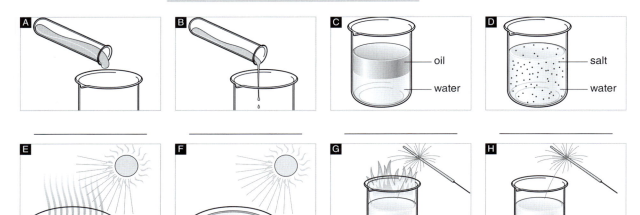

### Some important properties of petroleum products

#### Lubricating oil

Oils are in a viscous (or thick) liquid state at normal room temperature. They are immiscible (they cannot be mixed) with water. However, they are miscible (they can be mixed) with other oils.

**Viscosity:** The viscosity of a liquid is its thickness, stickiness or resistance to flow. The oil must be viscous enough to maintain a lubricating layer on the moving parts of an engine but fluid (or free-flowing) enough to flow around the engine parts to keep them well coated under all conditions. The viscosity index indicates how much the oil's viscosity changes as temperature changes. A higher viscosity index indicates that the viscosity changes less when the temperature changes. A lower index shows that the viscosity changes more when the temperature changes.

**Pour point:** This is the lowest temperature at which the oil can be poured out of a container or pumped around an engine. If the temperature falls below the pour point, the oil is too viscous to flow. A low pour point is useful because we want engines to start up easily in cold temperatures.

**Flash point:** This is the lowest temperature at which the oil gives off vapours which are flammable (able to ignite or catch fire easily). It is dangerous for the oil in a motor to ignite and burn, so a high flash point is desirable.

#### Jet fuels

Two types of jet fuel are used in aviation: avtag (aviation turbine gasoline) and avtur (aviation turbine kerosene). These fuels must have three properties. First, they must be free from impurities. Secondly, they must have a low viscosity index. Thirdly, they must be stable (not volatile) at high temperatures. Volatile liquids evaporate more quickly when heated, whereas stable liquids do not evaporate quickly.

**Language**

**Adjectives: prefixes**

| Adjectives give information about nouns. | a flammable/stable/viscous liquid |
|---|---|
| We can often make the opposite of an adjective by adding a prefix, e.g. **im-**, **un-**, **in-**. | miscible → **im**miscible<br>stable → **un**stable<br>correct → **in**correct |

**2** Complete this table with the adjectives in the box in 1.

| Property | | Opposite | |
|---|---|---|---|
| Adjective | Noun | Adjective | Noun |
| 1 _____ | viscosity | 5 _____ | fluidity |
| 2 _____ | miscibility | 6 _____ | immiscibility |
| 3 _____ | flammability | 7 _____ | non-flammability |
| 4 _____ | volatility | 8 _____ | stability |

**3** ▶ 24 Listen and check your answers in 2.

**4** Rewrite these sentences using the words in brackets.

When petrol evaporates, the gas can be ignited very easily. (flammable)
*When petrol evaporates, the gas is flammable.*
1  Oil floats on the surface of the sea because it is immiscible. (cannot/mixed/water)
2  This oil has a high viscosity index. (remains/viscous/high temperatures)
3  We need to buy an oil which has a low pour point. (can/poured/easily/cold)
4  Jet fuels such as avtur must not evaporate at high temperatures. (low/volatility)
5  This oil is too dangerous because it has a low flash point. (can/ignited/low/temperature)

**Writing** **5** Complete this text with the headings in the box.

Objective    Procedure    Result

## Water content or 'crackle' test

(1) _____
The purpose of the crackle test is to discover if there is any water in a sample of oil.

(2) _____
The method is as follows: first, a hot plate is heated to 135°C. Secondly, the oil sample is shaken vigorously to make the water molecules spread equally through the oil. Finally, a small amount of oil is dropped onto the hot plate using a clean dropper.

(3) _____
If no crackling is heard and no bubbles of vapour are seen after a few seconds, the oil is free of water. However, if bubbles are seen or crackling is heard, there is some water in the oil.

**6** Rewrite the text in 5. Use the imperative or *you* + verb.

*The purpose of the crackle test is to discover if there is any water in a sample of oil. First, heat/you heat a hot plate to 135°C.*

# Storage

Reading **1** Read this article. Which three factors are important when choosing an underground storage site?

Natural gas, a colourless, odourless, gaseous hydrocarbon, may be stored in a number of different ways. It is most commonly held underground under pressure in three types of facilities. These are: (1) depleted reservoirs in oil and/or gas fields, (2) aquifers and (3) salt cavern formations. Natural gas is also stored in liquid form in above-ground tanks. Each storage type has its own physical characteristics and economics, which influence how it is used. Two of the most important characteristics of an underground storage reservoir are its capacity to hold natural gas for future use and the rate at which gas inventory can be withdrawn – its deliverability rate.

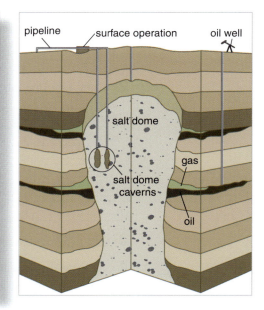

Vocabulary **2** Find words in the article in 1 that match these definitions.

1 having no smell _____
2 emptied out _____
3 water-bearing rock _____
4 large cave _____
5 all the material in storage _____
6 taken out _____

**3** Gas and gas storage facilities can be measured in different ways. Match 1–6 to a–f to complete the definitions.

**Storage measures**

1 Total gas storage capacity is the maximum volume of gas that
2 Total gas in storage is the volume of storage in the underground facility
3 Base gas (or cushion gas) is the volume of gas in a storage reservoir which is needed to maintain adequate
4 Working gas capacity refers to total gas storage capacity
5 Working gas is the volume of gas in the reservoir above the level of base gas. Working gas is available
6 Deliverability is a measure of the amount of gas that can be delivered (withdrawn) from

a) at a particular time.
b) minus base gas.
c) can be stored in an underground storage facility.
d) to the marketplace.
e) a storage facility on a daily basis.
f) pressure and deliverability rates throughout the withdrawal season.

mcf = million cubic feet
mmcf = bcf = billion cubic feet
mcm = million cubic metres
bcm = billion cubic metres

**4** Complete this table using the information in 3.

| Total capacity (bcf) | Base gas (bcf) | Working gas (bcf) | Working gas capacity (bcf) | Total gas in storage (bcf) |
|---|---|---|---|---|
| 7,563 | 3,728 | 2,473 | 1 _____ | 2 _____ |

## Language

### Compound nouns

| A **compound noun** is made up of two or more nouns. Some are written as two words and some as one word. | *storage reservoir* *marketplace* |
|---|---|
| The first noun normally indicates what type of thing the second noun is. | *working gas, base gas, cushion gas* (types of gas) *gas inventory* (a type of inventory) *gas storage capacity* (a type of storage capacity) Note: *total gas storage* = the total storage *total gas in storage* = the total gas |

**Speaking** **5** Work in pairs. Discuss the difference(s) between the following.

1 cushion gas/gas cushion
2 wall paper/paper wall
3 workbook/book work
4 safety helicopter/helicopter safety
5 test apparatus/apparatus test

**Listening** **6** ▶ 🎧 25 Listen to a conversation about storage measures in a facility in North America. Which types of storage are mentioned?

**7** Listen again. What do these numbers refer to?

1 123 _____
2 2,657 bcf _____
3 24,464 mmcf _____
4 30 million _____

**Speaking** **8** Work in pairs. Student A, look at the information on this page. Student B, look at the information on page 77. Follow the instructions.

**Student A**
You own the following gas storage facility and you want to sell it. Answer the telephone.

**Type:** salt caverns

**Number of caverns:** 7

**Capacity:** 135 mcm

**Base gas:** 45 mcm

**Deliverability:** 18 mcm/day

# Contamination control

**Listening** **1** ▶ 🔘 **26** Label this illustration with the phrases in the box. Then listen to part of a presentation about contamination control and check your answers.

> compressor/metering/regulation stations (×2)   end users   processing plants
> pipeline inspection gauge receivers   production plants   underground storage

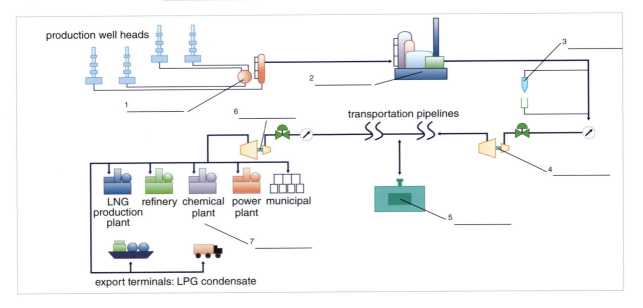

production well heads

1 _____
2 _____
3 _____
4 _____
5 _____
6 _____
7 _____

transportation pipelines

LNG production plant   refinery   chemical plant   power plant   municipal

export terminals: LPG condensate

**2** Listen again and write one or more examples of each of the following. Then read audio script 26 on page 73 and check your answers.

1 solid contaminant: _____
2 liquid contaminant: _____
3 typical problem(s) that contaminants can cause: _____

**Reading** **3** Read this information sheet and label diagrams A–C on page 49.

> Three common ways of removing contamination from pipelines are pipeline inspection gauges, filters and coalescers.
>
> 1 A pipeline inspection gauge is a device that scrapes the walls of the pipe. It cleans the deposits from the pipe as it moves along it.
>
> 2 A filter allows liquid to flow through but stops solid particles.
>
> 3 There are two main types of coalescers. Liquid–gas coalescers are used to separate water and hydrocarbon liquids from gas. Liquid–liquid coalescers separate liquid contaminants such as water from liquid products.

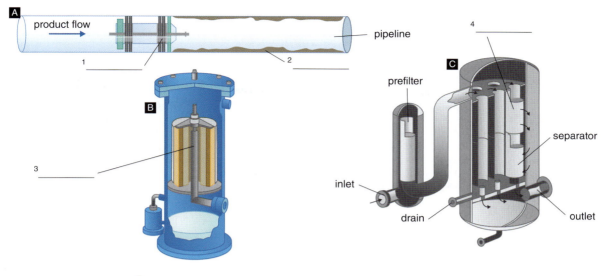

product flow

pipeline

1 _____

2 _____

3 _____

4

prefilter

separator

inlet

drain

outlet

**Vocabulary** **4** Complete this text with the words in the box.

> contamination   filters   filtration   liquid   pipelines

Most pipeline systems use a combination of techniques to prevent or reduce (1) _____ . For example, (2) _____ are often used to collect the solids removed after a pipeline inspection gauge has been through a pipe.

Pipeline inspection gauges are very common but cannot be used on all (3) _____ . In such cases, (4) _____ systems can be used to remove contaminants from the (5) _____ before it enters the pipeline.

**Language**

### Vague language

Sometimes we use **vague language** when we want to give people an impression of something without going into all the facts and details.

*We're talking about **things like** rust and pipe scale. These contaminants can cause **all sorts of** problems. They can lower the quality of the product **quite a bit**.*

**5** Read audio script 26 on page 73 and underline examples of vague language.

**Speaking** **6** Work in pairs. Student A, look at the information on this page. Student B, look at the information on page 77. Follow the instructions.

**Student A**
You work for a company called JK Pipelines. Student B, who works for a bank, is visiting your company today. Read this email from your boss and follow his/her instructions.

As you know, we have some important visitors today. I will be showing them around one of the metering stations later this morning but, unfortunately, I am not available to meet them when they arrive. Please meet them for me and give them a ten-minute introduction to pipelines. Keep things simple – as far as I know, they do not have a technical background.

# Transport of dangerous goods

**Speaking**

**1** Work in small groups. Can you drive? Do you have a driving licence? What extra skills do you need in order to drive a tanker? Discuss.

driving licence (BrE)
driver's license (AmE)

**Listening**

**2** ▶ 🔊 **27** Listen to a driving instructor talking about a training course. What type of course is it? What sorts of things will it cover?

**3** Listen again and choose *yes* (Y) or *no* (N) for each of these questions. Then read audio script 27 on page 73 to check your answers.

1 Are the rules the same in every country? (Y / N)
2 Is there a written test? (Y / N)
3 Will emergencies be covered on the course? (Y / N)
4 Is a placard necessary *only* at the front and rear of the vehicle? (Y / N)
5 Is there an emergency telephone number in the shipping documents? (Y / N)

**Reading**

**4** Read this extract about shipping documents and label the diagram with the words in the box.

diamond   hazard   shipping   sides   telephone

### SHIPPING DOCUMENTS (PAPERS)

The shipping document contains the four-digit ID number preceded by the letters *UN* or *NA*, the proper shipping name, the hazard class or division of the material(s) and, where appropriate, the Packing Group. The shipping document will also display a 24-hour emergency response telephone number.

| EMERGENCY CONTACT 1-000-000-000 | | **Example of emergency contact**<br>**(1) _____ number** |
|---|---|---|
| | **(2) _____ class**<br>**or division number** | |
| NO. AND TYPE OF PACKAGES | | QUANTITY |
| 1 TANKTRUCK    UN1219 | ISOPROPANOL    3    II | 12,000 LITRES |
| **ID number** | **(3) _____ name** | PACKING GROUP |

### Example of placard and panel with ID number

The four-digit ID number may be shown on the (4) _____-shaped placard or on an adjacent orange panel displayed on the ends and (5) _____ of a cargo tank, vehicle or rail car.

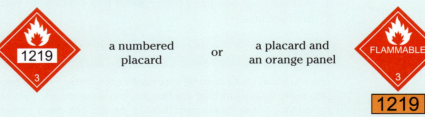

a numbered     or     a placard and
placard               an orange panel

Vocabulary **5** Match 1–7 to a–g to make collocations.

| | | | |
|---|---|---|---|
| 1 | shipping | a) | materials |
| 2 | hazardous | b) | group |
| 3 | hazard | c) | users |
| 4 | diamond- | d) | licence |
| 5 | driving | e) | class |
| 6 | packing | f) | shaped |
| 7 | road | g) | document |

Language

---

**Abbreviations**

| We often use **abbreviations** (the short forms of words) when we speak or write. | hazardous materials → hazmat<br>shipping documents → shipping docs<br>identification number → ID number<br>commercial driver's license → CDL |
|---|---|

---

**6** These abbreviations have been used in this book. What do they stand for?

1 LPG _____

2 E&P _____

3 SOP _____

4 MFP _____

5 DWT _____

Speaking **7** Work in pairs. Student A, look at the information on this page. Student B, look at the information on page 78. Follow the instructions.

**Student A**

Read these details about a training course and answer Student B's questions. Then swap roles. Ask Student B about his/her course.

*How long is it?*

*What will I learn on the course?*

*Who is the course for?*

---

# Dangerous goods regulations – Initial

Learn about shipping dangerous goods and the procedures, regulations, responsibilities and best practices involved.

**Course details**

Available as: classroom and in-company course
Duration: 5 days (40 hours)
Recommended level: entry-level and professional
Prerequisites: none

**What you will learn**

Upon completing this course, you will have the skills to:
- prepare and process dangerous goods shipments.
- understand legal requirements, operational restrictions and governing entities.
- champion dangerous goods compliance standards in your organisation.
- identify weak links in your handling procedures.
- examine safety issues and apply them appropriately in the workplace.

**Who should attend**

- airline acceptance staff, shippers and freight forwarders
- cargo training and development specialists
- ground handling and load control staff involved in the cargo chain
- regulatory compliance specialists
- personnel from the Departments of Transportation and Civil Aviation Authorities
- operations and station managers

# Impact

- describe incidents
- understand causes of accidents
- complete incident report forms
- handle oil spills

## Incidents

**Speaking**   **1**   Look at this photo. What type of installation is on fire?

**Listening**   **2**   ▶ 🎧 28   Listen to a report about an incident that took place at the Texaco Refinery, Milford Haven, Wales, on 24 July 1994. Answer these questions.

1  Was anyone injured?
2  What exploded?

3  What on-site damage occurred?
4  What off-site damage occurred?

**3**   Listen again and put the events in the correct order.

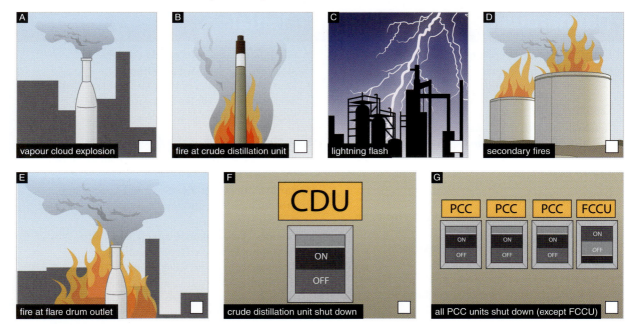

A  vapour cloud explosion

B  fire at crude distillation unit

C  lightning flash

D  secondary fires

E  fire at flare drum outlet

F  CDU · ON OFF · crude distillation unit shut down

G  PCC PCC PCC FCCU · ON OFF · all PCC units shut down (except FCCU)

**4**  ▶ 🌐 29  Listen to a conversation. What are the people talking about?

**5**  Listen again. What four errors are mentioned?

**Vocabulary**  **6**  Match 1–5 to a–e to make collocations.

| | | | |
|---|---|---|---|
| 1 | sustain | a) | a cloud |
| 2 | cause | b) | injuries |
| 3 | provide | c) | a fire |
| 4 | form | d) | damage |
| 5 | suffer | e) | feed |

**7**  Complete these sentences with the correct form of the collocations in 6.

1  There were no deaths in the incident but 26 people _____ .
2  The smoke from the fire _____ over the refinery.
3  The lightning strike _____ .
4  Several units _____ in the fire.
5  The crude distillation unit _____ to the PCC units.

**Language**

**Collocations with _fire_**

| Verb + _fire_ | start a fire, cause a fire, control a fire, contain a fire, put out/extinguish a fire<br>Note: If something **catches fire**, it starts to burn. (e.g. The building **caught fire**.) |
|---|---|
| _Fire_ + verb | A **fire broke out** at the refinery.  A **fire started** when lightning struck.<br>The **fire spread** quickly.  A **fire occurred** last night in a factory.<br>The **fire went out** after a few hours. |
| Compound nouns with _fire_ | fire brigade, fire risk, fire equipment, fire alarm, fire fighter, fire extinguisher, fire incident |
| Adjective + _fire_ | secondary fire, serious fire, small fire, large fire, hydrocarbon fire |
| Compound adjectives with _fire_ | **fireproof** material, **fire-retardant** jacket, **fire-resistant** clothing |

**8**  Complete this article with the words in the box.

burn  extinguished  fire  spread  started

The (1) _____ incident occurred at approximately 4.40 hours, according to reports from on-site personnel. As they were tripping out the drill string from the ground, the bit cleared from the hole, went up through the annular BOP and passed through the deck of the drilling rig, at which time the incident occurred. Fire (2) _____ in the immediate area around the drilling hole and (3) _____ upwards throughout the rig. The fire continued to (4) _____ freely until well control personnel were able to regain down-hole pressure and kill the well with water weighted with mud. The fire response team then (5) _____ the remaining fires.

**Speaking**  **9**  Work in pairs. Student A, look at the information on page 68. Student B, look at the information on page 78. Follow the instructions.

# Equipment problems

**Vocabulary** **1** Label photos A–C with the words in the box.

LPG loading arms    LPG storage tanks    LPG road tanker

_____    _____    _____

**Reading** **2** Read this extract from a report about an incident at an LPG road tanker loading facility in a refinery. Tick ✓ the most likely cause of the accident.

1 ☐ The driver did not tighten the connector.
2 ☐ The connection thread was worn.
3 ☐ The driver over-tightened the connector.

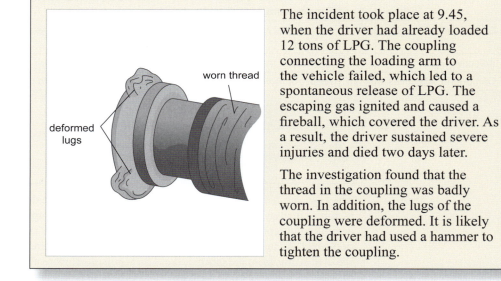

worn thread

deformed lugs

The incident took place at 9.45, when the driver had already loaded 12 tons of LPG. The coupling connecting the loading arm to the vehicle failed, which led to a spontaneous release of LPG. The escaping gas ignited and caused a fireball, which covered the driver. As a result, the driver sustained severe injuries and died two days later.

The investigation found that the thread in the coupling was badly worn. In addition, the lugs of the coupling were deformed. It is likely that the driver had used a hammer to tighten the coupling.

**Vocabulary** **3** Find words in the text in 2 that match these definitions.

1 not planned _____
2 started burning _____
3 surrounded _____
4 inquiry _____
5 a piece of equipment which connects two things _____
6 misshapen _____

**Vocabulary** **4** Complete this table with words from the text in 2.

| Verb | Noun |
|---|---|
| investigate | 1 _____ |
| 2 _____ | ignition |
| couple | 3 _____ |
| 4 _____ | failure |
| release | 5 _____ |
| 6 _____ | deformation |
| connect | 7 _____ |

**Language**

**Explaining why something happened**

| This led to ... | **This led to** a release of LPG. |
|---|---|
| This caused ... | The released hydrocarbons formed a vapour cloud, which ignited. **This caused** a major hydrocarbon fire. |
| The cause of ... was ... | **The cause of** the LPG release **was** the failure of the threaded coupling. |
| ... was caused by ... | The deformation **was caused by** hammering the lugs. |
| ... resulted in ... | A combination of errors **resulted in** the release of hydrocarbons. |
| ... as a result of ... | The unit was shut down **as a result of** the fire. |

**5** Complete this conversation with the words in the box. There is one extra word.

cause   caused   corrosion   hole   ignited   led   released   was

A: So let me get this straight: there (1) _____ a fire, and the fire (2) _____ to an explosion.

B: No, no ... the other way round.

A: Pardon?

B: The explosion caused the fire. The fire didn't (3) _____ the explosion. The explosion came first.

A: OK. And what (4) _____ the explosion?

B: Leaking gas. There was a(n) (5) _____ in the pipe. Gas leaked out, formed a cloud and then (6) _____ .

A: I see. And what caused the hole in the pipe?

B: That's what we don't know. We think maybe it was (7) _____ . But we'll have to wait for the investigation to be sure.

A: Fair enough.

**Listening** **6** 🔊 **30** Listen and check your answers in 5.

**Vocabulary** **7** Rewrite these sentences, inserting the missing words.

1 There was a fire. This led to explosion.
2 The fire caused explosion.
3 The fire led an explosion.
4 The report stated that the cause death was a heart attack.
5 As a result the accident, all drivers received additional safety training.
6 The fire caused by an electrical storm.
7 The fire resulted a number of injuries.

**Speaking** **8** Work in pairs. How would you prevent an accident like the one in 2 re-occurring? Make a list of recommendations.

*Check the thread couplings currently in use.*

# Doing the paperwork

**1** Read this extract from accident/incident reporting regulations. Find words and phrases that are related to injury.

---

The regulation applies to liquid hazardous materials pipelines. An accident report is required for any of the following:

1 an explosion or fire not intentionally set by the operator
2 the loss of 50 or more barrels (eight or more cubic metres) of hazardous liquid
3 the escape to the atmosphere of more than five barrels (0.8 cubic metres) a day of highly volatile liquids
4 the death of any person
5 bodily harm resulting in one or more of the following:

a) loss of consciousness
b) the necessity of carrying the person from the scene
c) the necessity for medical treatment
d) disability which prevents the discharge of normal duties or the pursuit of normal activities beyond the day of the accident

6 estimated property damage, including the cost of clean-up and recovery, the value of lost product and damage to the property of the operator or others, or both, exceeding $50,000.

---

**2** Do these incidents on a pipeline system need to be reported according to the regulations in 1? Choose *yes* (Y) or *no* (N).

1 a fire at a compressor station, resulting in two operators being treated for burns (Y / N)
2 a leaking valve, resulting in a small pool of oil underneath the valve (Y / N)
3 an explosion at a metering station, resulting in the death of two operators (Y / N)
4 the fracture of a pipe, resulting in the loss of 400 barrels of oil (Y / N)

**3** Read the extract from an incident report form below and find words or phrases that match these definitions.

1 deaths _____
2 people who have nothing to do with the pipeline _____
3 the time at a particular location _____
4 taken to another place _____
5 extra _____

---

11 Were there fatalities?  ◯ Yes ◯ No
   If *Yes*, specify the number in each category:
   11a operator employees  /___/___/___/___/
   11b contractor employees working for the operator  /___/___/___/___/
   11c non-operator emergency responders  /___/___/___/___/
   11d workers working on the right-of-way but NOT associated with this operator  /___/___/___/___/
   11e general public  /___/___/___/___/
   11f total fatalities (sum of the above)  /___/___/___/___/

12 Were there injuries requiring inpatient hospitalisation?
   ◯ Yes ◯ No
   If *Yes*, specify the number in each category:
   12a operator employees  /___/___/___/___/
   12b contractor employees working for the operator  /___/___/___/___/
   12c non-operator emergency responders  /___/___/___/___/
   12d workers working on the right-of-way but NOT associated with this operator  /___/___/___/___/
   12e general public  /___/___/___/___/
   12f total injuries (sum of the above)  /___/___/___/___/

13 Was the pipeline/facility shut down due to the incident?
   ◯ Yes ◯ No ⇨ Explain: _____
   If *Yes*, complete Questions 13a and 13b. (Use local time, 24-hour clock.)
   13a local time and date of shutdown  /___/___/___/___/ /___/___/ /___/___/ /___/___/
                                hour        month    day    year
   13b local time pipeline/facility restarted  /___/___/___/___/ /___/___/ /___/___/ /___/___/  ◯ still shut down
                                hour        month    day    year  (*supplemental report required)

14 Did the gas ignite?  ◯ Yes ◯ No
15 Did the gas explode?  ◯ Yes ◯ No
16 number of general public evacuated  /___/___/,/___/___/___/
17 time sequence (Use local time, 24-hour clock.)
   17a local time operator identified incident  /___/___/___/___/ /___/___/ /___/___/ /___/___/
                                hour        month    day    year
   17b local time operator resources arrived on site  /___/___/___/___/ /___/___/ /___/___/ /___/___/
                                hour        month    day    year

**Language**

| Telling the time: the 24-hour clock | |
|---|---|
| 07.00 | *oh seven hundred* |
| 16.00 | *sixteen hundred/sixteen hundred hours* (not *sixteen o'clock*) |
| 16.15 | *sixteen fifteen* (not *sixteen fifteen o'clock*) |

**Listening**   **4**   🔊 **31**   Listen to a conversation between two workers about an incident. What happened?

**5**   Listen again and complete the form in 3.

*Examples:*
*00.00 = midnight = /0/0/0/0/*
*08.00 = 8:00 a.m. = /0/8/0/0/*
*12.00 = noon = /1/2/0/0/*
*17.15 = 5:15 p.m. = /1/7/1/5/*
*22.00 = 10:00 p.m. = /2/2/0/0/*

**6**   🔊 **32**   Listen and complete this report with the correct times.

From what I understand, this is what happened: at (1) _____ the safety officer issued a hot work permit to two employees – two welders. The permit was valid from (2) _____ to (3) _____ in the afternoon. The task was to weld a handrail to the stairs on storage tanks 387 and 388. All the preparation work had been done the day before. The welders took a break at around (4) _____ and returned to work at around (5) _____ . They were unable to restart the engine on their welding machine, so they called maintenance. At around (6) _____ a maintenance truck gave their welding machine a jump start. At around (7) _____ an explosion occurred in tank 387, followed a minute later by an explosion in tank 388. Both welders were killed. Another tank in the area, 392, was damaged but did not catch fire. The firefighters were called at (8) _____, arrived at (9) _____ and had extinguished the flames by (10) _____ .

**Writing**   **7**   Read the report in 6 again and complete this hot work permit.

**Hot work permit**

Date: *6 Jan*

Valid from: (1) _____ to: (2) _____

Location: (3) _____

Name(s): *H Jahar, ID Vijay*

Job description: (4) _____

_____

Signed: *K. Zammit*

Job title: (5) _____

# Cleaning up

Speaking **1** Work in pairs. What are the main causes of oil spills?

Listening **2** 🔊 **33** Listen to a person talking about oil spills. Compare what he says with your answer in 1.

**3** Listen again and complete these phrases.

    1 routine operations such as _____, loading or unloading
    2 mishaps and collisions between vessels or tankers and other transportation _____
    3 ships running _____
    4 ruptured _____
    5 oil _____ activities
    6 mechanical failure of oil collection and _____ equipment

Reading **4** Look at this photo of an oil spill kit. Can you identify any of the items? How do you think these items are used? What else might an oil spill kit contain?

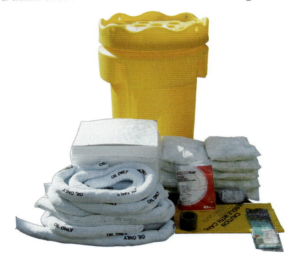

1 pound = 0.454 kg
curb (AmE) = kerb (BrE)

**5** Read this extract from procedures for spill prevention control and countermeasures (SPCC) and check your answers in 4. What type of spill is the extract about?

## Planning and preparation

Spill kits have been established at oil storage locations subject to SPCC regulations. The amount of spill materials kept at each location depends on the volume of oils stored there. Spill kit materials can be used for two main purposes: to absorb spilled oils and to block their flow.

The absorbents are of two types: diatomaceous earth (Oil Sorb) and polypropylene. Oil Sorb is supplied in 25-pound paper bags. Polypropylene is supplied as socks, pillows and pads. The use and limitations of each are described below:

| Absorbent type | Use | Limitations |
| --- | --- | --- |
| **Oil Sorb** | Spread on the leading edge of an oil spill and work back to the source. | Can absorb its weight in oil. Will absorb both water and oil. Does not float on water. |
| **Polypropylene** | Spread on the leading edge of an oil spill and work back to the source. | Can absorb 25 times its weight in oil. Will only absorb oil. Will float on water even if saturated with oil. |

Blocking materials are also of two types: sandbags and elastomer mats and berms. The use and limitations of each are described below:

| Blocking material | Use | Limitations |
| --- | --- | --- |
| Sandbags | Place in path of flow and butt the ends of the bags tightly to each other to form a barrier. | Getting a good seal between adjacent bags and the ground can be difficult. Use absorbent to catch leakage. Each bag weighs about 70 pounds and thus is difficult for some to move. |
| Elastomer mats | Place over storm or sanitary drains to seal them. | May not completely cover some larger drains. May not form a perfect seal on rough surfaces or along curbs. |
| Elastomer berms | Place in the path of flow to form a barrier or lay around drain openings to form a barrier. | May not completely encircle some larger drains. May not form a perfect seal on rough surfaces or along curbs. |

**Vocabulary** **6** Match 1–6 to a–f to make collocations.

| | | | |
| --- | --- | --- | --- |
| 1 | rough | a) | seal |
| 2 | drain | b) | edge |
| 3 | paper | c) | surface |
| 4 | perfect | d) | opening |
| 5 | leading | e) | bag |
| 6 | spill | f) | kit |

**7** Match words 1–7 to definitions a–g.

| | | | |
| --- | --- | --- | --- |
| 1 | butt | a) | nearby, neighbouring |
| 2 | leading edge | b) | soaked |
| 3 | curb | c) | front part |
| 4 | adjacent | d) | weaknesses |
| 5 | limitations | e) | push |
| 6 | saturated | f) | stones/concrete along the edge of a street |
| 7 | absorb | g) | take in |

**Language**

**Be supplied**

The phrase *be supplied* collocates with different prepositions.

| | |
| --- | --- |
| Oil Sorb **is supplied in** 25-pound paper bags. | Polypropylene **is supplied as** socks, pillows and pads. |
| The tool **is supplied with**/**without** a plug. | The kit **is supplied by** a company in Chicago. |
| Oxygen **is supplied to** the flame. | The software **is supplied on** a separate DVD. |

**8** Complete these sentences with the correct prepositions.

1 This area is supplied _____ gasoline from the Oston refinery.
2 Water is supplied _____ the blowdown drum to cool hot process steams.
3 Gas is supplied _____ most homes in this town.
4 The chemicals were supplied _____ powder.
5 Propane is also supplied _____ canisters.
6 Power is supplied _____ a 12-volt battery.
7 The mats are supplied _____ part of the spill kit.

**Speaking** **9** Work in pairs. Student A, look at the information on page 68. Student B, look at the information on page 78. Follow the instructions.

## 8

# Supply and demand

- **explain the process of buying and selling natural gas**
- **explain how oil is priced**
- **talk about trends**
- **discuss innovation in the oil industry**

## The markets

**Speaking** **1** Work in pairs. Where do industrial users in your country go to buy natural gas? Discuss.

**Reading** **2** Read the text and answer these questions.

1  What is the difference between on-system and off-system end users?
2  How do marketers get the gas to their customers?
3  Do pipeline companies sell natural gas in the USA? Why/Why not?

---

### How natural gas is traded

The diagram shows some of the types of natural gas transactions that take place as gas makes its way from the fields where it is produced to the end user.

The natural gas industry in the United States is highly competitive, with thousands of producers. Some producers market their natural gas and may sell it directly to local distribution companies or to large industrial buyers of natural gas. (Some of these large industrial buyers are 'on-system' end users, meaning that they receive physical natural gas deliveries from a local distribution company. Others are 'off-system' end users, meaning that they are directly connected to an interstate pipeline.) Other producers sell their gas to marketers who sell the natural gas in quantities that fit the needs of different types of buyers and who transport gas to their buyers. Marketers may be large or small and sell to local distribution companies or to commercial or industrial customers connected directly to pipelines or served by local distribution companies.

Most residential and commercial customers purchase natural gas from a local distribution company. In contrast, many industrial customers purchase natural gas from a marketer or producer instead of from the distribution company.

Note that pipeline companies do not buy and sell natural gas. Most of the major natural gas pipeline companies are federally regulated interstate pipeline companies. These companies are limited to providing transportation services, including storage. Thus pipeline companies move gas at government-regulated rates on behalf of buyers and sellers but do not participate in the buying and selling of natural gas.

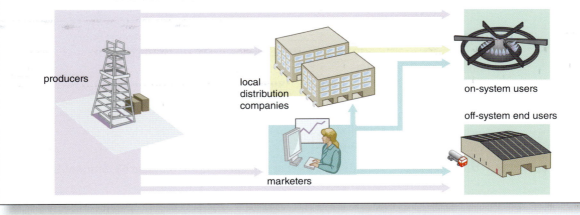

producers    local distribution companies    on-system users    off-system end users    marketers

---

**3** Match 1–7 to a–g to make collocations. Then find the collocations in the text in 2.

| | | | |
|---|---|---|---|
| 1 | highly | a) | customers |
| 2 | transportation | b) | company |
| 3 | federally | c) | services |
| 4 | interstate | d) | connected |
| 5 | directly | e) | competitive |
| 6 | distribution | f) | regulated |
| 7 | industrial | g) | pipeline |

**Listening**

**4** ▶ 🎧 34 Listen to a marketer explaining how he sells gas to his customers and complete these expressions with the words in the box.

> futures   spot   term

1 _____ price
2 longer _____ contract
3 _____ contract

**5** Listen again. Explain the meaning of the expressions in 4.

**Language**

---

**On behalf of someone/On someone's behalf**

| We use **on behalf of someone** to explain that we are doing something for someone else. | Pipelines move gas **on behalf of buyers and sellers**. I signed the letter **on behalf of my boss**. |
|---|---|
| We can also use **on someone's behalf** in the same way. | Pipelines move gas **on their behalf**. I signed the letter **on her behalf**. |

---

**6** Complete these sentences with the words in the box.

> behalf   my   of   on   our

1 Please don't do it _____ my behalf.
2 The distribution companies deliver the gas on behalf _____ the marketers.
3 On _____ of Mr Schultz, I would like to welcome you to the department.
4 I'm here on behalf of _____ crew.
5 We need an agent to get a good price on _____ behalf.

**Speaking**

**7** Work in pairs. Student A, look at the information on this page. Student B, look at the information on page 79. Follow the instructions.

**Student A**

You represent a power station. You need to buy natural gas to supply your turbines. Telephone Student B, a marketer, and discuss options for the delivery of the gas.

*What is an off-system end user?*
*Can I buy direct from the producers?*
*Do pipeline companies sell gas?*

# Prices

**1** Read the article about crude oil prices and answer these questions.

1 What is the difference between WTI and Brent Blend?
2 What do *light*, *sweet* and *sour* mean in relation to oil?
3 Which oil is sweeter: WTI, Brent Blend or OPEC Basket?

---

Crude oil prices measure the spot price of various barrels of oil, most commonly either the West Texas Intermediate or the Brent Blend. The OPEC Basket Price and the NYMEX Futures price are also sometimes quoted.

West Texas Intermediate (WTI) crude oil is of very high quality because it has a low density and a high proportion of light hydrocarbon fractions. It also has low sulphur content. For these reasons, it is often referred to as 'light', 'sweet' crude oil. These properties mean it is excellent for making gasoline, which is why it is the major benchmark of crude oil in the Americas.

Brent Blend is a combination of crude oil from 15 different oil fields in the North Sea. It is less 'light' and 'sweet' than WTI but still excellent for making gasoline. It is primarily refined in Northwest Europe and is the major benchmark for other crude oils in Europe or Africa. For example, prices for other crude oils in these two continents are often set as a differential to Brent (for example, Brent minus $0.50).

The OPEC Basket Price is an average of the prices of oil from Algeria, Indonesia, Nigeria, Saudi Arabia, Dubai, Venezuela and Mexico. OPEC uses the price of this basket to monitor world oil market conditions. OPEC prices are lower because the oil from some of the countries has higher sulphur content, making it more 'sour' and therefore less useful for making gasoline. Transportation distance is also a factor.

The NYMEX is the value of 1,000 barrels of oil, usually WTI, at some agreed upon time in the future. In this way, the NYMEX gives a forecast of what oil traders think the WTI price will be in the future.

---

**Vocabulary** **2** Match words 1–5 to definitions a–e.

1 benchmark
2 differential
3 proportion
4 value
5 average

a) relative quantity
b) monetary worth (how much money you get for this commodity)
c) amount of difference
d) a standard used for comparison
e) arithmetic mean (all items added together and then divided by the number of items)

**3** Complete these sentences with the words in 2.

1 The price _____ between Brent and WTI was only 50 cents.
2 The _____ price of a litre of gasoline was $3.45.
3 The market _____ of an oil tanker is in the tens of millions of dollars.
4 Heavy crude oils contain a high _____ of heavy hydrocarbons.
5 Brent Blend is used as a(n) _____ in Europe and Africa.

**Speaking** **4** Work in pairs. The market price depends on many factors, including the cost of production. What does it cost to produce a barrel of oil? Brainstorm some factors.

**Listening** **5** ▶ 🔊 **35** Listen to an employee from an exploration company talking about the costs for the drilling operations of an exploration project. Complete the percentages on this pie chart.

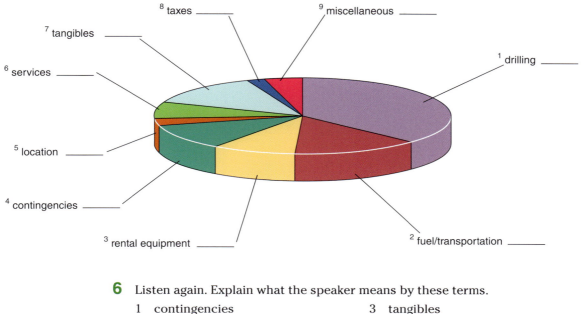

8 taxes _____    9 miscellaneous _____

7 tangibles _____

6 services _____

1 drilling _____

5 location _____

4 contingencies _____

3 rental equipment _____    2 fuel/transportation _____

**6** Listen again. Explain what the speaker means by these terms.

1 contingencies
2 services
3 tangibles
4 miscellaneous

### Language

| Phrasal verbs | |
|---|---|
| **Phrasal verbs** often consist of a verb + preposition. The meaning of the phrasal verb is often different to the meaning of the separate words. | *Brainstorm some **factors** with your partner.* (*factors* = noun, meaning 'items') *We normally **factor in** a contingency cost.* (*factor* = part of a phrasal verb, meaning 'include') |

**7** Complete these sentences with the correct form of phrasal verbs formed from the words in the boxes. All the phrasal verbs come from previous units.

clean   look   make   start   switch

after   on   out   up (×2)

1 It's dark in here. Please _____ the lights.
2 If the oil has a low pour point, the engine is easier to _____ in winter.
3 My job is to _____ the drilling equipment.
4 We are talking about the hydrocarbons that _____ oil and gas.
5 _____ the pipeline before use.

**Speaking** **8** Work in pairs. Student A, look at the information on this page. Student B, look at the information on page 79. Follow the instructions.

**Student A**
Ask Student B about the difference between WTI, Brent, OPEC and NYMEX prices. Then answer his/her questions.

# Trends and forecasts

**Listening** **1** ▶ 🔘 **36** Listen to a talk about OPEC's World Oil Outlook 2011 and match words a–g to 1–7 in the bar chart.

a) diesel/gasoil     d) naphtha     f) other products
b) ethane/LPG     e) jet/kerosene     g) residual fuel
c) gasoline

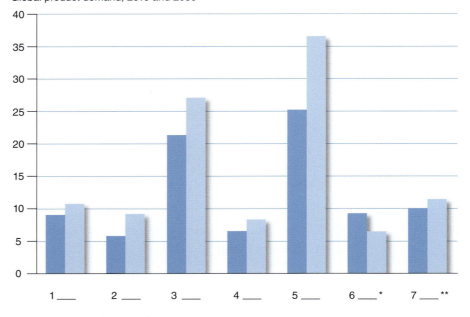

Global product demand, 2010 and 2035

*Includes refinery fuel oil.

**Includes bitumen, lubricants, waxes, still gas, sulphur, direct use of crude oil, etc.

**2** Listen again. What do *go up* and *go down* mean?

**3** ▶ 🔘 **37** Listen to five experts talking about trends in the oil and gas industry. Match speakers 1–5 to these topics.

a) shale gas ____
b) buying and selling companies ____
c) deepwater drilling ____
d) China as an importer of oil ____
e) natural gas ____

**4** Listen again and answer these questions.

1 How deep are E&P companies now drilling?
2 Why are there so many mergers, acquisitions and joint ventures?
3 Why does China need to import more oil?
4 Where are most of the world's natural gas reserves?
5 One reason for the success of shale gas is new technology. What is the other reason?

**Speaking** **5** Work in pairs. Do you agree with the trends mentioned in the recording? What other trends can you think of? Discuss.

**Language**

**6** Underline the adjectives and adverbs that describe trends in audio scripts 36 and 37 on page 75.

**7** Complete this text using the information in the graph.

This graph shows the outlook for (1) _____ in Alaska from 2008 to (2) _____ . As you can see, we start off in 2008 with 0.7 (3) _____ . This will drop steadily to 0.4 in (4) _____ . It will then (5) _____ to around 0.46 by 2022 and then (6) _____ to 0.28 in 2030. There will be another rise to around 0.41 in (7) _____ , followed by a drop to just (8) _____ 0.4 in 2035.

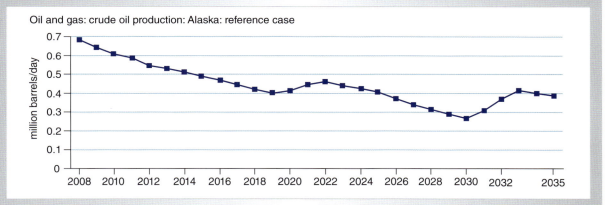

Oil and gas: crude oil production: Alaska: reference case

**Speaking** **8** Work in pairs. Student A, look at the information on this page. Student B, look at the information on page 79. Follow the instructions.

**Student A**
Describe this graph for Student B to draw. Then draw the graph Student B describes.

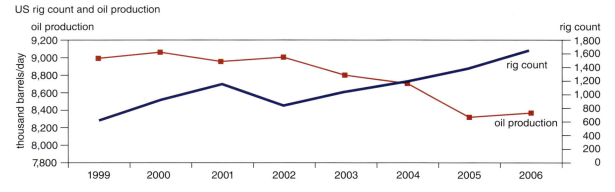

US rig count and oil production

# Innovation

Speaking **1** Read this quotation. Was the Sheikh right about fuel cell technology and the changes in the oil industry? What new technologies do you know about?

> '30 years from now there will be a huge amount of oil and no buyers. Oil will be left in the ground. The Stone Age came to an end, not because we had a lack of stones; and the Oil Age will come to an end, not because we have a lack of oil. [Fuel cell technology] is coming before the end of the decade and will cut gasoline consumption by almost 100 percent. On the supply side it is easy to find oil and produce it, and on the demand side there are so many new technologies, especially when it comes to automobiles.'
>
> *Sheikh Zaki Yamani, Oil Minister of Saudi Arabia (1962–1986), June 2000*

Reading **2** Read this programme from a conference on innovation in the oil and gas industry. What sessions would you be most interested in? Why?

| **Innovation in the oil and gas industry: Programme** | |
| --- | --- |
| 09.00 | Coffee and registration |
| 09.30 | Welcome address |
| | Keynote speaker: Harold J. Curtiss, CEO HJC Enterprises (main hall) |
| 10.30–11.00 | Coffee |
| 11.00–12.30 | **Session A** |
| | A1 Focus on floating production systems: lowering the costs (room 203) |
| | A2 Drilling rigs and quality control: our experience in Texas (room 208) |
| | A3 Natural gas storage: the case for salt caverns (room 304) |
| 12.30–13.30 | Lunch |
| 13.30–15.00 | **Session B** |
| | B1 Blowout preventers: what you need to know (room 203) |
| | B2 Deepwater exploration: where are we and where are we going? (room 208) |
| | B3 Perspectives on shale reserves (room 304) |
| 15.00–15.30 | Coffee |
| 15.30–17.00 | **Session C** |
| | C1 Pipelines and pipeline inspection gauges: old technology, new ideas (room 203) |
| | C2 Refinery maintenance: fewer shutdowns, more profit (room 208) |
| | C3 Transporting LPG: new regulations and what they mean (room 304) |
| 17.00–18.00 | Panel discussion (main hall) |
| | Representatives from leading E&P companies discuss innovation and answer your questions. |
| 19.30 | Dinner |

**Vocabulary** **3** Match words 1–5 to definitions a–e.

1 registration
2 keynote speaker
3 opening address
4 networking
5 panel discussion

a) making new contacts; sharing ideas and information
b) a formal conversation on selected topics in front of an audience, with selected speakers
c) someone who gives an important talk at a conference
d) the first talk at a conference
e) signing in to the conference

**Listening** **4** ▶ 38 Listen to two co-workers at the conference discussing the programme in 2 and tick ✓ the sessions they decide to attend.

| Session | Tony | Jane |
|---|---|---|
| A1 | | |
| A2 | | |
| A3 | | |
| B1 | | |
| B2 | | |
| B3 | | |
| C1 | | |
| C2 | | |
| C3 | | |
| Panel discussion | | |

**5** Listen again. Why doesn't Jane want to talk to Tony at the next coffee break?

**Language**

**Using *yes* to agree and disagree**

| Agreement | Yes, good idea./Yes, OK./Yes, definitely./Yes, exactly. |
|---|---|
| Partial agreement | Yes and no. |
| Disagreement | Yes, but ... |

**6** Underline all the phrases with *yes* in audio script 38 on page 75. Do they show agreement, partial agreement or disagreement?

**7** Disagree with the following statements. Start with *Yes, but ...* .

1 We should stop searching for fossil fuels and use more renewables.
2 Salaries in the oil industry are too high.
3 There is hardly any innovation in the oil industry – just the same old ideas.
4 Technology is the answer to all our problems.
5 There are too many accidents with deepwater drilling.

**8** Work in pairs. How do you think the following phrase is used in conversation?

*Let's agree to disagree.*

**Speaking** **9** Work in pairs. Your English lessons are coming to an end. Discuss the best way to continue learning in the future. Think of at least three options. Your partner can agree or disagree with what you say.

## 4 Equipment

**The blowout preventer**

**Speaking exercise 6 page 31**
Make notes about the function of the items in these photos. Then describe the items to Student B.

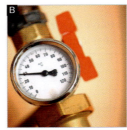

## 5 Project management

**In a meeting**

**Speaking exercise 7 page 37**
You are the project manager. Ask Student B, the supervisor, questions about the dismantling of the rig. You want to know if all the tasks in this list have been done yet.

1 Detach the kelly from the travelling block.
2 Uninstall the power system.
3 Take down all the electric cables.
4 Disconnect the mud pipes and hoses from the equipment.
5 Lower the derrick.
6 Dismantle the rig platform.
7 Fill in the mud and reserve pits.
8 Remove the equipment from the site.

## 7 Impact

**Incidents**

**Speaking exercise 9 page 53**
1 Read this incident report. Explain what happened to Student B. Answer his/her questions.
2 Student B will explain a similar incident to you. Ask questions to find out what happened. Use 2 on page 52 to help you.

On 23 February 1999 a fire occurred in the crude unit at Tosco Corporation's Avon oil refinery in Martinez, California. Workers were attempting to replace piping attached to a 150-foot-tall fractionator tower while the process unit was in operation. During removal of the piping, naphtha was released onto the hot fractionator and ignited. The flames engulfed five workers located at different heights on the tower. Four men were killed and one sustained serious injuries.

**Cleaning up**

**Speaking exercise 9 page 59**
Explain to Student B how sandbags, elastomer mats and elastomer berms are used in the event of an oil spill. Use the words in the box.

butt   cover   drains   encircle   place   rough surfaces   seal

# Audio script

## Unit 1 People and jobs

▶ 🔊 02

**1**  A:  What do you do exactly?
   B:  Well, my specific job at the moment is optimising lube oil production. We blend different oils and we use additives to get the right properties in the products. When we're happy with the product, we transfer it to large storage tanks. From there it's pumped into barrels or bottles and sent to the customer.

**2**  A:  Is it an easy job?
   B:  Easy job? No! It's hard, physical and very dirty! We normally work for 12 hours at a time in all weathers – painting, cleaning, carrying, you name it. All the other people on the crew, from driller to motorhand to derrickman, started as roustabouts. It's normal in this industry.

**3**  A:  Do you work in a crew?
   B:  Well, I'm part of the production support team, so I move around from rig to rig. I work with different crews on different rigs, sometimes inside an office and sometimes outdoors.
   A:  And the job is mainly technical?
   B:  Yes, but I also have to work with people, co-ordinating and managing. So my job isn't only technical. And of course there are a lot of health and safety procedures to follow as well.

**4**  A:  So where do you work?
   B:  I'm a geophysicist at Erbgos. I'm based in Anchorage.
   A:  A geophysicist? Er … what does that mean exactly?
   B:  Well, in my case, I work in a team. We're responsible for finding out what's under the surface, so things like types of rock, different layers, where the oil is and so on. Basically, we use vibrator trucks to send shock waves into the ground, and receivers to pick up the reflected waves from the different layers. My job is to analyse the data.

▶ 🔊 03

[Ab = Abdul; H = Harish; J = John; M = Mohammed; Al = Ali; S = Samir]

Ab: Hello, and welcome to the rig. I'm Abdul Suleman.
H:  Harish. Harish Baijal.
Ab: I'm afraid Mr J is away today, visiting JK Enterprises.
H:  JK Enterprises? In Aberdeen?
Ab: Yes, that's right. They're the exploration company that hired the rig.
H:  I see.
Ab: The rest of us work for Ali Basri under contract. Let me introduce you to the crew. Here we have John Gregory, in charge of all things mud.
J:  Hi.
H:  Hi. Harish. I'm the new medic.
J:  First time on a rig?
H:  Er … yes. It looks complicated.
J:  Ah, you'll get used to it.
Ab: And this is Mohammed. He runs the drilling crew which goes on shift in about ten minutes. Right, Mohammed?
M:  Yes, that's right. Hi, Harish. Welcome. And if you'll excuse me, off to work I go!
Ab: And this is Ali. He is responsible for all the engines on the rig.

H:  Pleased to meet you.
Al: Likewise.
Ab: And finally we have Samir, who reports directly to Mr J. Samir is responsible for all the technical stuff, while I look after the crews and support staff.
S:  Hello.
H:  Hi.
Ab: How about a cup of tea? Then I'll take you out to meet the crew coming off shift. And after that I'll show you the quarters and the sick bay.
H:  Great, thanks.

▶ 🔊 04

**1**  A:  On this rig, workers are on the job for 12 hours a day for seven straight days. Then they get a week-long break.
   B:  Ah, that's different to my old rig. We operated in three-week shifts. So three weeks on the rig and three weeks off.
   A:  That's hard.
   B:  Yes. The night shifts were the worst but the breaks were great!

**2**  A:  We do routine tests and non-routine tests. For routine tests, we take samples at specific times from specific locations, according to a set schedule. This is an important part of the quality control programme in the refinery.
   B:  What about non-routine tests?
   A:  Ah … we do those when something out of the ordinary happens, for example, equipment breakdown or maintenance.
   B:  I see.
   A:  For example, last week we had a problem with some of the crude inflow, so we had to reschedule all our tests.
   B:  Did you manage it?
   A:  Yes, but it was hard work. Long hours.
   B:  Do you work shifts at this refinery?
   A:  Some people do, yes. But I don't. I'm on call 24 hours a day, seven days a week.

**3**  A:  My company specialises in gas pipeline repair and maintenance. Last week was a typical week.
   B:  What did you do?
   A:  Well, we did a job here in Germany. The job was to install a new pipe liner and also to replace some flanges. We spent the first week getting things ready. Everything had to be planned properly to minimise downtime.
   B:  I see. And what happened next?
   A:  It all went according to plan. The operators shut down a four-mile section of underground pipe. We only had three days, so we had to work around the clock to complete the job, which meant three shifts. As supervisor, I was at work, or at least available for work, the whole time.
   B:  Did you finish on time?
   A:  Actually, we finished two hours early. And next week we're doing the same thing on a different section.
   B:  Sounds very interesting.
   A:  Yes, always a different location.

**► 05**

A: OK, have a look at this map. You can see the coast here, with the mouth of the river here. And here are two islands, just north-east of the mouth.
B: Yep, OK.
A: The scale is 1:63,360, so one inch is a mile.
B: OK.
A: Now, this is the plan: the refinery will be here, on the east side of the mouth. We can't use the west side because the tankers will need the harbour here, just opposite the larger island, and we want to be as close as possible. This means that the pipeline is quite short, only about a mile from the refinery, to the west side of the harbour.
B: Why not put the refinery closer to the harbour?
A: Good question. Basically, this area here, around the harbour, is a fishing village. So we don't want to get too close.
B: I see.
A: Now the rigs. The plan is to have three platforms at first. Each platform will be named after one of the director's daughters. So we have Platform Sally here, just east of the small island. We have Platform Debbie here, in between the two islands, and we have Platform Marjorie here, in the middle of the mouth of the river.
B: OK.

## Unit 2 Procedures

**► 06**

1 jewellery
2 flammable items
3 temporary
4 rotary table
5 regularly

**► 07**

1 A: OK, before we start the drilling, we should clean all the equipment. We don't want any cross-contamination.
B: What should I use? The steam cleaner?
A: Yes, that's fine. And afterwards wash it with potable water.
B: Potable?
A: That means drinkable water.
B: Ah. OK.
2 A: We shouldn't use any newly painted tools for this job.
B: Why not?
A: The paint chips off and goes into the monitoring system.
B: Right.
3 A: Make sure you throw your old gloves away – before you touch the clean equipment.
B: These should be OK. They're only slightly dirty.
A: No, throw them away. Even slightly soiled gloves contaminate.
B: OK.
4 A: See this rope? It's porous, so we can't decontaminate it properly.
B: I see.
A: It should be thrown away.
B: OK, boss. No problem.
5 A: Before we leave base camp, all the equipment should be thoroughly cleaned.
B: That's a lot of work.
A: Yep, so better get started!
B: OK.

**► 08**

[S = Supervisor; R = Roustabout]
S: Right, now let me give you some general rules about working with loads. Listen carefully. First of all, make sure the work area is clear. If there's an obstruction, remove it. And by obstruction I mean anything which shouldn't be there: tools, equipment, boxes – you name it. OK?
R: OK.
S: Good. Next, always check the condition of the equipment. If you see any damage, just tell me. For example, corroded or broken wire ropes, or worn slings. That kind of thing is very dangerous. Understand?
R: Yes, OK.
S: Always use taglines to control a load. If a load swings to the left or right, you just pull it back. And another thing: attach hooks or shackles to pick-up points. If there are no pick-up points, use slings and packing to prevent damage.
R: Got it.
S: Now, do you know the emergency stop signal?
R: Yes. Like this?
S: Yes, exactly. Well, if you see a problem, give the signal.
R: OK.
S: Oh, yeah. If you aren't a qualified rigger, you mustn't rig loads.
R: Aha, OK.
S: And finally, if you don't understand your task, ask the person in charge.

**► 09**

1 A: I visited Platform Sally yesterday.
B: Oh yes? How did it go?
A: No problems. The weather was bad, so we went by boat.
B: Rough?
A: Yes. Very rough. The hardest part was getting onto the boat in the harbour. There was a missing rung on the ladder and I nearly fell in the water ... It's not funny! I could have died!
B: Or maybe just got very wet!
2 A: Sorry I'm late. Had a bit of an accident.
B: Really? Where?
A: On the derrick.
B: The derrick? What happened?
A: I went up to have a look at the block. There was a broken monkeyboard, believe it or not! I twisted my ankle.
B: Ouch! You OK?
A: It's OK now but I was not a happy man, I can tell you. And the derrickhand was not a happy man either, after I finished with him. A broken monkeyboard! I could have fallen!
3 A: Did you hear what happened yesterday? At the airfield?
B: No, what?
A: Some idiot forgot he was wearing a cap. On the pad.
B: So?
A: So the cap got blown away by the rotors.
B: Whoops!
A: Yes. Whoops! The idiot ran after it. He nearly lost his head near the tail rotor!
B: What? Everyone knows not to wear loose clothing on an airfield!
A: Yes. And that's not the worst thing.
B: Why? What happened?
A: The idiot was me! And I might have to see the boss.
B: Oh no!

# Unit 3 Processes

### ▶ 🔊 10

A: Can you tell me how oil fields are formed?
B: Yes, of course. It's really very simple. First you have organic matter which falls to the sea bed.
A: Organic matter is things like plants and animals?
B: Yes, exactly. Next, this organic matter gets covered by sediments, such as clay or sand. Over time, more and more sediments fall, so we end up with different sedimentary layers.
A: And the pressure increases?
B: Yes, and the temperature increases too. And this process converts the organic matter into hydrocarbons; in other words, oil and gas.
A: I see.
B: Now this oil and gas is in what we call the source rock. After a while it flows upwards to what we call the reservoir rock. And finally, it stops in a so-called geological trap.
A: Why do you call it a trap?
B: Because it can't flow upwards any more. The cap rock, which is above the reservoir and is impermeable, stops the oil and gas escaping to the surface. It traps the oil and gas.
A: I see.
B: There are different types of traps, of course. Look at these diagrams. The first one is an anticline. You can see it's shaped like a dome. Here you can ...

### ▶ 🔊 11

1   sedimentary layers
2   hydrocarbons
3   reservoir rock
4   geological trap
5   impermeable

### ▶ 🔊 12

1   Jet fuel is made from kerosene, which condenses between 175 and 325 degrees.
2   When naphtha vapour is cooled to between 60 and 100 degrees, it condenses.
3   Diesel oil is produced by cooling crude oil vapour to between 250 and 350 degrees.
4   The boiling point of industrial fuel oil ranges from 370 to 600 degrees.

### ▶ 🔊 13

Good morning, everyone, and thanks for coming to this presentation. My objective in this talk is to explain some of the processes in oil refining. I'd like to start by saying a few things about hydrocarbons. ...
... That brings me to the three main processes: cracking, reforming and alteration. Let's look at cracking first. ...
... Now let's move on to reforming. ...
... And thirdly, let's turn to alteration. ...
... As the flow chart shows, the next process is treatment. ...
... As shown in the flow chart, after treatment we have blending. ...
... And finally, I'd like to mention some of the products of refining. ...

### ▶ 🔊 14

1   A: So can you tell me more about the pipeline laying process?
     B: Yes, sure. We use different types of vessels, depending on the job. If we're in deep water, we normally use a pipe-trenching barge behind the lay barge.

A: Did I understand you correctly? You use trenches in deep water?
B: Sorry, I mean shallow water, not deep water. In deep water we use a gravel-dumping vessel. It covers the pipe with gravel because it's too deep to dig a trench.
A: Ah, I see.
2   A: We waterproof the pipes offshore.
     B: Pardon?
     A: With bitumen and concrete.
     B: Offshore? On the lay barge?
     A: Oh sorry, my mistake. Onshore. Not offshore.
3   A: And what does the stinger do?
     B: The stinger? The stinger is used to guide the gravel.
     A: So in other words, the stinger places the gravel in the right place?
     B: Oh. No ... not the gravel. I meant the pipeline, of course. As we lay the pipeline, the stinger is used to make sure that everything goes smoothly. For example, it stops the pipeline from bending and breaking.
     A: Thank you.

# Unit 4 Equipment

### ▶ 🔊 15

1   Tension leg platforms are more rigid than fixed platforms.
2   Fixed platforms are more flexible than compliant towers.
3   Fixed platforms are the smallest platforms and operate in the shallowest waters.
4   Tension leg platforms are larger than sea star platforms.
5   Spar platforms can operate in deeper water than tension leg or sea star platforms.
6   All of the platforms move sideways in storms, except fixed platforms.

### ▶ 🔊 16

One of the most dangerous accidents during the drilling and production stages of a well is a blowout. This is an uncontrolled flow of oil, gas or water at high pressure out of the well. The blowout preventer, or BOP, is designed to shut down the well quickly in an emergency blowout. It prevents fluids from escaping under extreme pressure. The BOP is located between the drilling platform and the ground. It is operated remotely by means of hydraulic pistons. There are three main types of blowout preventer: annular, blind ram and shear ram. Don't worry, I'll explain what these mean in a minute. But very briefly, in this diagram, the annular preventer is at the top, the blind rams are below that and the shear rams are at the bottom. Because these are stacked on top of each other, we sometimes call this a BOP stack.

### ▶ 🔊 17

The pumps suck the drilling mud out of the mud pits. They then pump the fluid through a hose to the rotary equipment. From the rotary hose the fluid enters the swivel and the kelly. It then flows down through the drill string. Then it leaves the drill bit and flows around the annulus. The fluid picks up pieces of rock and sand. Then the mud rises up the well hole between the drill pipe and the casing. At the top of the well, the fluid flows through the mud return line into the shaker. The shaker takes the cuttings out of the fluid. The fluid then goes into the mud pits again and the cuttings enter the reserve pit.

### ▶ 🔊 18

[K = Kevin; R = Rob]
K: Hello? Hello? Can you hear me?
R: Hello? Yes, I can hear you. Is that you, Kevin?
K: Yes, yes! Hi, Rob. Bad connection!
R: Yes.

K: Pardon?
R: I said yes.
K: Are you at the terminal?
R: Yes, yes I am.
K: Good. Have you checked the gauges yet?
R: No, no, I haven't. I just arrived.
K: OK. Call me when you check them, please. I think we have a problem. We're getting some funny readings here at the control station.
R: I can't.
K: You can't? What? You can't check the gauges? Why not?
R: I can check the gauges. But I can't call you. My battery is almost dead.
K: Ah! Didn't you check the battery before you left?
R: No, I didn't. I forgot. Sorry.
K: Ah, OK. I'll send Jack out.
R: Pardon?
K: I'll send Jack out. With new batteries.
R: OK. That's great. Thanks.
K: Don't mention it! Just check the gauges, OK?
R: OK. Will do.

# Unit 5 Project management

▶ 🔊 19

A: Hello, Hamish. How are you getting on? Have you raised the derrick on the platform yet?
B: Yes, we have.
A: Great. When did you assemble the rig platform?
B: Let's see. Yes, we assembled it in the first week of February.
A: So are you installing the lifting and rotary system now?
B: Yes, we are.
A: What else are you doing now?
B: We're setting up the tanks and pumps, and connecting the pipes and hoses.
A: OK. That's good. When will you string the electrical cables?
B: We'll do that in the second week of March.

▶ 🔊 20

1  A: OK, guys. Here's the plan: we can't use the helicopters because of the fog. So we're going to go out to the rig by bus and boat. The bus will be here in about an hour, so you all have time to grab a cup of coffee. It's going to be a long day.
   B: How long will the drive take?
   A: About three hours, I guess. And then the boat will take another six or seven hours on top of that.
   B: It'll be dark when we get there.
   A: Maybe, yes. I'll amend the schedule on the bus. We'll start the inspections tomorrow morning.
   B: OK.

2  Welcome, everybody, and thanks for coming. As you know, this meeting is basically to discuss the new schedule for the refinery visits. Now, I know this is very unusual but this project comes straight from the minister. There have been several refinery shutdowns in the last few months, both planned and unplanned, and the result has been shortages in various products. Diesel oil has been in very short supply, for example. The minister is not happy and has asked for a full report. So this office will be visiting all refineries in the country to check exactly what is happening on the ground. We'll be handing in our report exactly seven weeks from today. After that it's back to normal. I'll be leaving tomorrow morning for a meeting with the minister, so I wanted to discuss the schedule with you before I go.

3  A: OK, so the next item on the agenda is the drilling equipment packages for the ETW drill ships.
   B: Sorry, what ETW drill ships?
   A: Ah! Forgot you weren't here last week, Tony. It's a new contract. We're supplying drilling equipment packages, including pressure control equipment, for four drill ships belonging to ETW. It's a Brazilian company.
   B: Ah, OK, thanks. Sounds good.
   A: Yes, it is. The contract was signed last week and we're starting deliveries next month. In fact, Harry is flying out next week and I'll be joining him just before the first delivery.
   B: Four packages. Must be worth a bit.
   A: It's the biggest order in the company's history, so it's pretty good. And I understand there are more orders on the way, so …

▶ 🔊 21

[Jo = Joe; Ja = Jack; T = Tom]
Jo: OK, moving on to Pipeline Emerald, it looks like our planned route is no longer possible. The impact on the environment is just not acceptable – too much damage to vegetation, historic sites, wildlife and so on. I'll send you the full report. So now we're looking at alternatives. The first option is to use pipeline systems we already have. Jack, any thoughts?
Ja: Yes, this is a possibility. But existing pipelines won't give us the capacity we need without more money, more investment. We'll need to expand the facilities, new compressor stations, valve stations, communication towers, you name it. Probably a lot more expensive than the original route.
Jo: Hm … OK. Can you do the maths, please? I'll need facts, even if in the end we simply say no to the idea.
Ja: Sure, no problem. If I start my team on it today, you'll have something on your desk by, say, next Monday. How does that sound?
Jo: Great, thanks. The second option is to look at other routes. This area to the north is unacceptable for geological reasons – there are too many faults. But this area to the south looks quite good. Tom, any comments?
T: Yes, we looked at that area last year when we did the original planning. If I remember correctly, we'll need to cross a lot of water.
Jo: Yes, that's right. It's mostly wetlands … but still possible.
T: Yes, yes, of course. Definitely feasible. And there was another issue …
Jo: Go on.
T: Yes, the area to the south doesn't have many roads or towns. If we build a pipeline there, we'll have to build access roads and housing for the workers. Probably around five to six hundred people, which is quite an impact. OK, the housing will be temporary and we'll take it away afterwards, but still …
Jo: Yes, that's a good point. Thank you.

▶ 🔊 22

[T = Tom; J = Joe]
T: Hi, Joe, it's Tom.
J: Hi, Tom. How's it going?
T: Good, thanks. Listen. I wanted to discuss the water crossings for the new pipeline. In the wetlands. I've been reading the regulations. Got some good news.
J: Go on.
T: OK, well, you know that in this area they classify three types of water bodies, right? Minor water bodies, like streams and so on, which we can cross using normal open-cut methods.

J: Yep.

T: Secondly, major water bodies, which we'll have to cross using HDD – horizontal directional drilling, you know.

J: Yes, yes. I got that, OK.

T: The third category is intermediate water bodies, OK? That's something between minor and major.

J: OK.

T: Now here's the thing: if we want to cross intermediate water bodies, we'll have to divert the water – you know, using dams and pumps or flumes. Except if we work in the dry season. If we work in the dry season, we'll be able to use open-cut methods. A lot cheaper.

J: Hm ... yes, I see what you mean. So let me get this right. Basically, if there's no water flow, we'll be allowed to use open cut?

T: Yes, exactly. So if we time things right, we'll save a lot of money.

J: Yes, yes, that's excellent! Good news indeed.

### ▶ 🔄 23

OK, let's look at the project scope. This project really consists of three main elements. First of all, we're looking at a new tanker jetty to replace the current one. Basically, the new jetty will be able to handle tankers of up to 50,000 DWT instead of 12,000. Secondly, we want to expand the bulk fuel storage facility. The expansion will include bunded storage tanks as well as a new customer collection facility. The capacity will increase from 80,000 m³ to 189,000 m³ and we'll be able to store seven different product types. And thirdly, we're looking at a new pipeline system to transfer fuel from the jetty to the storage facility. This will replace the old system and, hopefully, follow the same route. I say 'hopefully' because we haven't finished our survey yet.

## Unit 6 Products

### ▶ 🔄 24

1 viscous – viscosity
2 miscible – miscibility
3 flammable – flammability
4 volatile – volatility
5 fluid – fluidity
6 immiscible – immiscibility
7 non-flammable – non-flammability
8 stable – stability

### ▶ 🔄 25

A: We have 123 sites in the USA. Most of them are aquifers and salt caverns but we also have a few depleted reservoirs. Our working gas capacity is 2,657 bcf and our daily deliverability is 24,464 mmcf.

B: Sorry, could you tell me what *mmcf* stands for?

A: Sure, no problem. *M* stands for 'one thousand'. So *mm* is a million.

B: I see. And *bcf* is one billion cubic feet?

A: Yes, that's exactly right. You got it.

B: And one last question. Could you tell me about costs?

A: Oh, I'm sorry. I don't really know much about that. You'll have to ask Pete when he comes back.

B: Thank you.

A: But I can tell you that the last salt cavern facility that we commissioned costs around 30 million dollars per bcf of working gas capacity, give or take a little. I know because I read the report yesterday. But as I say, you're better off asking Pete for specific details.

B: I see. Thank you.

### ▶ 🔄 26

Here we have a diagram showing the process of getting the product to the customer. Starting at the production well heads in the top left, we move to the production plants and the processing plants. After that, we have the P.I.G. receivers – that's pipeline inspection gauge receivers – on the right here. And then the various stations in the pipeline: compressor, metering and regulation stations. Sometimes we have underground storage facilities, shown here, just under the transportation pipelines. Then there are more compressor, metering and regulation stations. And finally, we get to the various end users. OK so far? Good. Now, what I want to do today is tell you something about contamination in the system and, in particular, the pipeline system. As you probably know, we have two main types of contamination: solid and liquid. Solid contaminants include things like black powder, which is a term for all the corrosion that takes place in any pipeline system. So we're talking about stuff like rust and pipe scale. Liquid contaminants are things like water, glycols, hydrocarbon condensates, as well as compressor oils. And these contaminants can cause all sorts of problems, such as corrosion, erosion, blockages and so on.

### ▶ 🔄 27

Welcome to the course. OK, now I know that some of you have transported dangerous goods in the past but, as you know, every country is different, so I want to go over some of the main rules. The first thing, which I am sure you all know, is to explain why we are here. In this country you have to pass an extra test before you can transport dangerous goods. We call this a hazmat endorsement – *hazmat* stands for 'hazardous materials'. And you also need a tank endorsement if you want to drive a vehicle which needs a class A or B CDL and has a tank to carry liquids or gas. *CDL* stands for commercial driver's license. I'll give you the exact details later.

The point is, to get those endorsements, you must pass a test. A written test. The training will be in this building, mostly on this floor. The practical training will be done on the hard standing in front of Building 7, which is where we have all the vehicles, as well as on the road. During the week we'll be looking at a number of topics, including bulk tank loading and unloading, driver responsibilities, parking rules, dealing with emergencies and so on. The full list and schedule is in your file.

Let's go over some of the basics. The system we use to warn other road users is very simple. Each vehicle has four placards, which are these diamond-shaped signs you can see here. Each side of the vehicle has to have a placard, so that's front, rear and both sides. The important thing is that they're easy to see. If you carry dangerous goods, you will also have the shipping documents. These documents have the identification number of what you are carrying, as well as an emergency telephone number in case you have a problem. These documents must stay in the cab.

## Unit 7 Impact

### ▶ 🔄 28

[A = Alicia; TJ = Tom Jeffries]

A: We interrupt this programme to bring you some breaking news. An explosion, followed by a number of fires, occurred early this morning at the Texaco Refinery in Pembroke. 26 people sustained injuries on site, none serious. We go now to our reporter Tom Jeffries, who is on site. Tom, can you tell us what happened?

TJ: Hi, Alicia. Well, it seems that the whole incident started during an electrical storm early this morning. A lightning strike hit the crude distillation unit that provides feed to the Pembroke Cracking Company units. This caused a fire and the unit was shut down by staff at the refinery. During the course of the morning, all the other PCC units except the FCCU were shut down. *FCCU* stands for 'fluid catalytic cracking unit', which is basically where the crude oil is turned into gasoline. What happened next is a little confusing. It seems that a combination of errors resulted in the release of 20 tonnes of flammable hydrocarbons from the outlet pipe of the flare knock-out drum of the FCCU. This formed a vapour cloud which ignited and exploded. The explosion caused a major fire at the flare drum outlet itself, as well as a number of secondary fires. Alicia.

A: Thank you, Tom. What can you tell us about damage to the refinery?

TJ: Well, the refinery suffered quite severe damage to process plant, buildings and storage tanks. But the refinery is well away from centres of population, so off-site damage is very limited.

### 🔊 29

A: The report mentions a combination of errors. Could you tell me more about that?

B: Well, you know that later in the morning we shut down the PCC units?

A: Except for the FCCU.

B: Right. Except for the FCCU. Big mistake. Well, after the PCC units were shut down, we thought that everything would be OK. But there were a couple of other issues we didn't know about. First of all, a control valve was shut but the control system said it was open.

A: I see. So there was a problem with the control system?

B: Yes, exactly. And we didn't have an overview of the whole process. The control panel allowed us to look at different elements but not everything together. So the operators were only looking at the known problem areas. They didn't see the big picture.

A: Ah … What about alarm systems?

B: Yes, we had those. But so many different alarms were going off that it wasn't easy for the two operators to work out exactly what was happening. In the last few minutes before the explosion there were nearly 300 alarms going off. And as I said, the biggest mistake was to try and keep the FCCU running when it should have been shut down.

### 🔊 30

A: So let me get this straight: there was a fire, and the fire led to an explosion.

B: No, no … the other way round.

A: Pardon?

B: The explosion caused the fire. The fire didn't cause the explosion. The explosion came first.

A: OK. And what caused the explosion?

B: Leaking gas. There was a hole in the pipe. Gas leaked out, formed a cloud and then ignited.

A: I see. And what caused the hole in the pipe?

B: That's what we don't know. We think maybe it was corrosion. But we'll have to wait for the investigation to be sure.

A: Fair enough.

### 🔊 31

[R = Robin; Y = Yusuf]

R: Hey, Yusuf. How's it going?

Y: Robin! Welcome back!

R: So what's new?

Y: Well, we had a fire while you were away.

R: Really? When?

Y: Friday the eleventh.

R: Wow! That's amazing! The eleventh of the eleventh of 2011?

Y: Yes.

R: Don't tell me it happened at eleven o'clock!

Y: No, no, it didn't. That would be too much of a coincidence!

R: Anyone hurt?

Y: Yes. One person. Do you know Suresh Mishra? He works in the control room.

R: Yes, I do.

Y: He was burnt quite badly, I think. They took him to hospital by helicopter. There was also a party of university students visiting but, from what I heard, they were all OK. Around 20 of them – quite a large group. Anyway, they were evacuated straight away, of course.

R: Do you know when they'll open the pipeline again?

Y: Well, Duncan thinks maybe early next week. But it depends on what they find.

R: When did they actually shut everything down?

Y: Pretty quickly, I think. Suresh radioed the control room straight away. So 20.00, give or take a couple of minutes. I know the time because the football had just started.

R: You and your football! What was the score?

Y: 3–1.

R: Was it just a fire? Or did the gas explode?

Y: Just a fire. Suresh was burnt while he was trying to put it out.

R: He should have waited for the fire brigade.

Y: Yep. They were there by 20.30, I heard.

### 🔊 32

From what I understand, this is what happened: at 14.30 the safety officer issued a hot work permit to two employees – two welders. The permit was valid from 14.30 to 18.40 in the afternoon. The task was to weld a handrail to the stairs on storage tanks 387 and 388. All the preparation work had been done the day before. The welders took a break at around 15.45 and returned to work at around 16.05. They were unable to restart the engine on their welding machine, so they called maintenance. At around 16.15 a maintenance truck gave their welding machine a jump start. At around 16.50 an explosion occurred in tank 387, followed a minute later by an explosion in tank 388. Both welders were killed. Another tank in the area, 392, was damaged but did not catch fire. The firefighters were called at 16.53, arrived at 17.09 and had extinguished the flames by 18.45.

### 🔊 33

Oil spills? Let's see. Well, a lot of oil is spilled during routine operations such as refuelling, loading or unloading, that sort of thing. Then there are mishaps and collisions between vessels or tankers and other transportation vehicles. Those are the ones that often get in the news. Er … ships running aground is another one. Then we have ruptured pipelines at sea or on land. And oil exploration activities, drilling and so on. And of course, there's also mechanical failure of oil collection and storage equipment.

## Unit 8 Supply and demand

### 🔊 34

Yes, so most of my transactions are done on the phone or the internet. I negotiate with the buyer and agree a price for the gas. I also arrange delivery to a specific location on their behalf. This is called a spot price, and fluctuates depending on supply and demand. Some customers like longer term contracts so that they know that their gas will be delivered over a period of time. The price is not fixed beforehand but again depends on the market. A futures contract is different. Here the price is fixed when the contract is agreed. This means that the buyer and seller are locked into a price – both sides know exactly how much the gas will cost.

## 35

A: OK, let's see: a typical breakdown for our drilling operations? Well, let's look at this project here, which will give you an idea. Our biggest cost is always the drilling costs. This covers payments to the drilling contractors for the rig and the people who do the drilling. Costs here can vary, depending on the area and the type of rig. In this project it was around 37 percent.

B: What about fuel? To run the rig, I mean.

A: Well, we calculate that separately. In this case it was 14 percent. That includes running the rig, as well as moving it to and from the location.

B: Ah, I see. OK.

A: Now the drilling costs don't cover all the equipment we have to rent, so things like mud processing equipment, monitoring equipment, forklifts, pumps and so on come under rental equipment. In this project it was nine percent of the total cost. Then we have another big cost, which is contingencies.

B: You mean emergencies and things?

A: Well, not only emergencies. Just things we don't foresee. Like bad weather, for example, or stuck drill strings and so on. We always factor in a contingency cost.

B: Always the same?

A: No, no, not at all. If we have a difficult location, the contingency cost will be higher, or if we have an inexperienced crew or very deep wells. It varies, depending on how we see the risk. In this project, it came to 11 percent.

B: OK.

A: Then we have smaller costs. The location cost – in this project, three percent – covers the costs to prepare the site for drilling – levelling, for example, and adding a foundation for the drilling equipment. Service costs – here, seven percent – cover other things we have to buy, like drill bits, drilling mud and so on.

B: Aren't things like that included in the drilling costs?

A: No, not always. It varies. But in this project they were additional costs.

B: I see.

A: And then, of course, there are the tangibles like pipe casing and tubing. These are directly related to the price of steel on the world market. In this project it came to 13 percent.

B: OK.

A: And that's about it. Oh, sorry. There's also taxes. Around two percent. And of course, miscellaneous, around four percent, which covers all the things we haven't covered in the other sections.

B: Like?

A: Let's see … um … permits, insurance, legal fees, communications, that sort of thing.

B: OK. That's all very clear. Thank you.

## 36

As you can see from this bar chart, we have divided the products into seven main types. The dark blue column shows demand in 2010 and the light blue column shows 2035. The highest demand is clearly for diesel and gasoil, projected to rise to 37 million barrels per day in 2035. This is quite a sharp increase. Next comes gasoline at 27. Both these products are directly related to the growth in road transport all over the world. The other five products are all around the ten million barrels per day mark. So we have ethane and LPG, around nine in 2010 but only a slight rise to around eleven in 2035, naphtha around six in 2010, rising to nine in 2035, and jet kerosene around seven, rising to eight. The only area which is set to decrease is residual fuel, which we think will drop slightly from nine to seven.

## 37

1 I think a major trend is the move towards more deepwater drilling. E&P companies are drilling down to more than 6,000 feet on a regular basis, trying to find those last remaining pockets of oil. So, as I say, for me the major trend is more deepwater drilling, which I think will increase significantly.

2 We've already seen a dramatic increase in the number of mergers, acquisitions and joint ventures in recent years, and this trend is set to continue. We're all trying to make our companies stronger in a difficult economic environment.

3 China's industrial and commercial demands have risen sharply and this trend will continue. China will continue to be one of the world's biggest importers of oil.

4 Natural gas is already the fastest growing energy source in the world and this will not change for the foreseeable future – and most of it is in Russia.

5 New technologies such as hydraulic fracturing and horizontal drilling, as well as the rising cost of conventional drilling, mean that shale gas will continue to play an increasingly important role.

## 38

[T = Tony; J = Jane]

T: White, one sugar, please. Thank you. Oh hi, Jane. Didn't see you there.

J: Hi, Tony. Good to see you.

T: Did you enjoy the opening address?

J: You mean Harold Curtiss? Well, he made some good points but I found him a bit difficult to understand.

T: Yes. Yes, you're right. He's always like that. I guess he needs to learn to speak a bit more slowly. His accent was very difficult.

J: Yes, exactly. He spoke like he had an apple in his mouth! Anyway, Session A next. The salt caverns should be interesting.

T: Yes, definitely. But the other two look good, too.

J: It's a shame we can't go to all of them.

T: Eh? Why not?

J: Oh Tony! The sessions are concurrent – A1, A2 and A3 are at the same time.

T: Oh! Are they? I thought they followed on from each other.

J: No. Look, they're in different rooms. Weren't you listening when they explained the programme at the beginning?

T: Well, in that case, it makes sense if we go to different sessions. That way we can report back on more sessions.

J: Yes, OK. Right, I'll do A3, the salt caverns, then.

T: OK, let's see. I'll go to A1, the FPS one, then.

J: Yes, good idea. Now Session B. You choose first.

T: Er … B1, blowout preventers for me, I think. No, wait. Er … yes, blowout preventers. Yes.

J: OK. I'll do B3, the shale gas, then. And then in Session C I'll go to C3, about the new LPG regs.

T: OK. Then I'll do C1, pipelines and pipeline inspection gauges.

J: Great. That's sorted, then. I guess I'll see you at the panel discussion.

T: Or at one of the coffee breaks. Or lunch.

J: Yes. But let's network, not just chat to each other. We're here to make new contacts, after all. We can compare notes next week in the office.

T: Yes, yes, of course.

## 2 Procedures

**Load handling instructions**

**Speaking exercise 7 page 17**

You are a new roustabout. Practise the conversation in 2 on page 16 with Student A. Then swap roles and repeat the activity. Remember to discuss the following:

- obstructions
- stop signals
- taglines
- condition of equipment

## 4 Equipment

**The blowout preventer**

**Speaking exercise 6 page 31**

Make notes about the appearance of the items in these photos and the materials they are made of. Then describe the items to Student A.

**Pipeline components**

**Speaking exercise 7 page 35**

You are an engineer at the control station. Listen to track 18 again and roleplay a similar conversation with Student A, a line walker inspecting a pipeline.

## 5 Project management

**In a meeting**

**Speaking exercise 7 page 37**

You are the supervisor. Read this list of tasks. The tasks with ticks ✓ have been done. The notes in brackets reflect your plan. Report to Student A, the project manager, and answer his/her questions.

| | |
|---|---|
| 1 Detach the kelly from the travelling block. ✓ | 5 Lower the derrick. ✓ |
| 2 Uninstall the power system. ✓ | 6 Dismantle the rig platform. *(today)* |
| 3 Take down all the electric cables. ✓ | 7 Fill in the mud and reserve pits. *(tomorrow)* |
| 4 Disconnect the mud pipes and hoses from the equipment. ✓ | 8 Remove the equipment from the site. *(next week)* |

**Presenting your idea**

**Speaking exercise 7 page 43**

1  Read this newspaper ad. What is it about? Discuss with Student A.

2  Look at this map of an aviation fuel delivery system for Vancouver International Airport. Find the elements in the key on the map. Then describe the delivery system to Student A.

> **Vancouver International Airport**
> will be holding a press conference tomorrow to present their plans for a new aviation fuel delivery system. The press conference will take place in Terminal 1 and will start at 10 a.m. Members of the public are welcome.

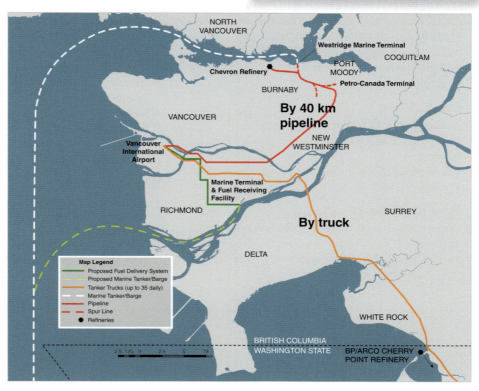

# 6 Products

**Storage**

**Speaking exercise 8 page 47**

You work for a company which needs to buy additional gas storage capacity. You have heard that Student A may have a facility for rent or sale. Call him/her and ask for information.

**Contamination control**

**Speaking exercise 6 page 49**

You work for a bank. Today you are visiting JK Pipelines, a company which operates pipelines. Your bank is thinking about investing in it and has arranged a fact-finding visit so that you can learn about its operations. Unfortunately, your colleague is ill, so you are alone. Just before you leave, you receive this email. Read it and meet with Student A, an employee of JK Pipelines, to find out about the company's operations.

> I've heard that contamination is a big problem for pipeline operators and this affects the quality of the product. Please find out as much as you can about how JK Pipelines deal with this. Thanks. Enjoy the visit!

| Transport of dangerous goods | **Speaking exercise 7 page 51** |
|---|---|

Student A has got information about a training course. Ask questions to find out about it. Then swap roles. Read these details about a training course and answer Student A's questions.

*How long is it?*
*What will I learn on the course?*
*Who is the course for?*

## IATA dangerous goods regulations (DGR) – Initial

Review IATA (International Air Transport Association) cargo dangerous goods regulations and understand the legality and the responsibility of shippers, agents and airlines.

### Course details

Available as: distance learning course
Duration: 35–45 hours for course, plus 3.5 hours for exam
Recommended level: entry-level and professional
Prerequisites: none

### What you will learn

Upon completing this course, you will have the skills to:

- apply the IATA cargo dangerous goods regulations correctly.

- discern the legal aspects and the responsibility of shippers, agents and airlines involved in transporting dangerous goods.
- identify and classify individual dangerous goods items.
- verify goods are properly packed, marked and labelled.
- fill in and check the 'Shipper's Declaration for Dangerous Goods'.

### Who should attend

- dangerous goods processing staff
- freight forwarders
- cargo agents
- shippers and operators staff preparing COMAT (Company Material)
- cargo operations managers and frontline supervisors

# 7 Impact

| Incidents | **Speaking exercise 9 page 53** |
|---|---|

1 Student A will explain an incident to you. Ask questions to find out what happened. Use 2 on page 52 to help you.
2 Read this incident report. Explain what happened to Student A. Answer his/her questions.

BP plc said a crude distillation unit (CDU) caught fire on 4 October at the 88,528-b/cd Lingen refinery in northwest Germany. One person was hospitalised. 'The fire was brought under control in about 30 minutes and damage was contained to that unit,' a BP spokesman in London said. 'The CDU that caught fire has been shut down but the refinery has a second CDU that remains operational,' BP said. The fire broke out while the unit was coming back after summer maintenance.

| Cleaning up | **Speaking exercise 9 page 59** |
|---|---|

Explain to Student A how polypropylene socks, pillows and pads, and diatomaceous earth (Oil Sorb) are used in the event of an oil spill. Use the words in the box.

| absorb | back | edge | float | source | spread | work |
|---|---|---|---|---|---|---|

# 8 Supply and demand

**The markets**

**Speaking exercise 7 page 61**

You work for a natural gas marketing company as a marketer. Your company supplies gas to a wide range of users, both commercial and industrial. Student A, a representative of a power station, is calling for information. Answer his/her questions.

**Prices**

**Speaking exercise 8 page 63**

Answer Student A's questions. Then ask him/her about typical costs in drilling operations.

**Trends and forecasts**

**Speaking exercise 8 page 65**

Draw the graph Student A describes. Then describe this graph for Student A to draw.

Btu = British thermal unit

Energy consumption in the United States, China and India, 1990 – 2035 (quadrillion Btu)

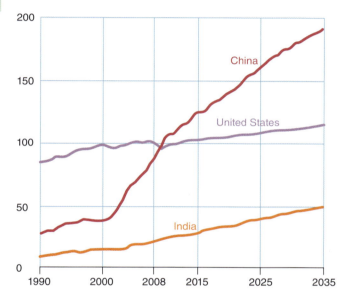

**Pearson Education Limited**
Edinburgh Gate
Harlow
Essex CM20 2JE
England
and Associated Companies throughout the world.

www.pearsonelt.com

© Pearson Education Limited 2012

The right of Evan Frendo and David Bonamy to be identified as authors of this Work has been asserted by them in accordance with the Copyright, Designs and Patents Act 1988.

First published 2012

ISBN: 978-1-4082-6995-4

Set in ITC Cheltenham Book
Printed by Graficas Estella, Spain

**Acknowledgements**
The publishers and author would like to thank the following people for their feedback and comments during the development of the material: Ludovic Lacan, UK; Richard Brettell, Suadi Arabia; Pamela Heath, Canada; Sotirios Koutsoukos, UK

We are grateful to the following for permission to reproduce copyright material:

**Figures**
Figure on page 50 adapted from 2008 Emergency Response Handbook, Transport Canada, the U.S. Department of Transportation, and the Secretariat of Communications and Transport of Mexico, p.2, with permission from Pipeline and Hazardous Materials Safety Administration (PHMSA); Figure on page 63 adapted from http://aepiworld.com/var/uploads/File/AFE%20Cost%20Breakdown.pdf; Figure on page 65 from U.S. Energy Information Administration; Figure on page 65 from International Energy Outlook 2011, DOE/EIA-0484(2011), Fig. 13, p.10 (EIA 2011), U.S. Energy Information Administration.

**Text**
Extract on page 14 adapted from Standard Operating Procedure Nine, Drilling Methods, SOP 2150, Version 2.0 (3/18/2003) S, DENR, with permission from South Dakota Department of Environment and Natural Resources; Extracts on page 46 adapted from The Basics of Underground Natural Gas Storage, U.S. Energy Information Administration (US EIA 2004); Extract on page 50 adapted from 2008 Emergency Response Handbook, Transport Canada, the U.S. Department of Transportation, and the Secretariat of Communications and Transport of Mexico, p.2, with permission from Pipeline and Hazardous Materials Safety Administration (PHMSA); Extract on page 51 adapted from IATA DGR - Initial (Category 6), http://www.iata.org/training/courses/Pages/tcgp03.aspx, © IATA 2012. All rights reserved, IATA Training and Development Institute; Extract on page 51 from Training Portfolio - IATA Dangerous Goods Regulations (DGR) - Initial, http://www.iata.org/training/courses/Pages/tcgp13.aspx, © 2012 International Air Transport Association. All rights reserved. Extracts of the IATA WEB SITE are reproduced within this Coursebook. The information contained in the English for the Oil Industry Level 2 Coursebook for Pack is subject to constant review in light of changing government requirements and regulations. No reader should act on the basis of any such information without referring to applicable laws and regulations and/or without taking appropriate professional advice. Although every effort has been made to ensure accuracy, neither IATA nor Pearson Education Ltd. shall be held responsible for loss or damages caused by errors, omissions, misprints or misinterpretation of the contents hereof. Furthermore, IATA and Pearson Education Ltd. expressly disclaim any and all liability to any person or entity, whether a purchaser of the English for the Oil Industry Level 2 Coursebook or not, in respect of anything done or omitted, by any

such person or entity in reliance on the contents of that publication or of extracts reproduced herein; Extract on page 53 adapted from Forensic Fire Investigation Case: Oil and Gas Drilling Rig Fire, http://www.kevinkennedyassociates.com/cold-forensic-fire-investigation-case-oil-and-gas-drilling-rig-fire, with permission from Kevin Kennedy Associates, Inc; Extract on page 53 adapted from BP reports refinery fires in Germany, Spain by OGJ Editors 10/06/2011, Houston, http://www.ogj.com/articles/2011/10/bp-reports-refinery-fires-in-germany-spain.html, with permission from Oil & Gas Journal; Extract on page 56 adapted from Regulatory Compliance Guide, Section 2, Compliance Guide No. DOT1, Revised 5/2004 130B, with permission from Pipeline and Hazardous Materials Safety Administration (PHMSA); Extract on page 56 from Incident Report - Gas Distribution System, Form PHMSA F 7100.1 (Rev. 06-2011), p.2, with permission from Pipeline and Hazardous Materials Safety Administration (PHMSA); Extract on page 57 from Instructions for completing form Incident Report - Gas Distribution System, Form PHMSA F 7100.1 (Rev. 06-2011), part A.2, with permission from Pipeline and Hazardous Materials Safety Administration (PHMSA); Extract on pages 58-59 adapted from Safe Operating Procedure, Spill Prevention Control and Countermeasures (SPCC) & Storm Water BMPs Spill/Release Preparation & Response (Revised 10/11), with permission from UNL Environmental Health and Safety; Unit 7, Lesson 1, Exercise 2 audio extract adapted from HSE Accident Reports, http://www.icheme.org/resources/safety_centre/publications/hse_accident_reports.aspx © Institution of Chemical Engineers 2012. Contains public sector information published by the Health and Safety Executive and licensed under the Open Government Licence v1.0; Unit 7, Lesson 4, Exercise 2 audio extract adapted from Oil Spills Response (BP Refinery, Kwinana, Western Australia 2012) courtesy of BP Refinery (Kwinana), Australia; Extract on page 62 adapted from About.com US Economy Crude Oil Prices Definitions by Kimberley Amadeo, About.com Guide, http://useconomy.about.com/od/economicindicators/p/Crude_Oil.htm. © 2012 Kimberley Amadeo (http://useconomy.about.com) Used with permission of About, Inc., which can be found online at www.about.com. All rights reserved. In some instances we have been unable to trace the owners of copyright material, and we would appreciate any information that would enable us to do so

**Photo ackowledgements**

The publisher would like to thank the following for their kind permission to reproduce their photographs:

(Key: b-bottom; c-centre; l-left; r-right; t-top)

**A. W. Wilde Photography:** photographersdirect.com 14 (E); **Alamy Images:** ableimages 14 (D), Calum Davidson 38 (A), David Hancock 17 (B), Design Pics Inc 54 (C), G P Bowater 23, Global Warming Images 42 (B), Ian Buswell 42 (A), Justin Kase zsixz 10 (B), Photoshot Holdings Ltd 38 (B), PHOVOIR 4 (D), SCPhotos 42 (C), Stuart Walker 54 (B), Svabo 5; **Bechtel:** 17 (E); **Corbis:** Steve Chenn 10 (A); **Courtesy of Associate Engineers, India:** 54 (A); **Courtesy of Vancouver Airport Fuel Facilities Corporation:** 43, 77; **DK Images:** Dave Rudkin 17 (A); **Fotolia.com:** alisonhancock 14 (B), Anna Khomulo 8, annaia 68 (C), corepics 9, Eduard Isakov 48, JEAN-MARC MEDINA 10 (C), Kadmy 4 (C), lightmoon 6, lightpoet 4 (A), photosoup 76 (B), Tomas Sereda 38 (C); **Courtesy of Industrial Training International, used with permission:** 17 (D); **Media Wales Ltd:** 52; **Pearson Education Ltd:** Gareth Boden 76 (A); **PhotoDisc:** 68 (A); **Photolibrary.com:** Redchopsticks 50; **Rex Features:** Jon Santa Cruz 14 (A); **Shutterstock.com:** 57, Frontpage 14 (B), Ingvar Tjostheim 4 (B), optimarc 17 (C), servantes 68 (B), Shi Yali 76 (C); **Yellow Shield Ltd:** 58

**Cover images:** *Front:* **Getty Images:** Mark A Leman / Stone l; **iStockphoto:** Christian Lagereek background; **SuperStock:** age fotostock r, Cultura Limited c

All other images © Pearson Education

Every effort has been made to trace the copyright holders and we apologise in advance for any unintentional omissions. We would be pleased to insert the appropriate acknowledgement in any subsequent edition of this publication.